STOP

PROCRASTINATING

An Easy-to-Follow Approach to Overcoming Procrastination, Building Self-Discipline, and Taking Action in Your Life
(2022 Guide for Beginners)

Grace Marshall

CONTENTS

INTRODUCTION

It is difficult to imagine that procrastination might have a positive side effect since everyone always speaks about the negative impacts of procrastination. The negative impacts are more visible since the whole workplace is aware when someone fails to meet an assignment deadline. However, delaying might be beneficial.

There is such a thing as deliberately delaying. This is when someone compiles a list of things to do, including the one item they don't want to do, and then completes everything else on the list but the one thing that absolutely must be completed. Eventually, the whole list is checked off, and the one thing that truly has to be done is staring you down. If you then do that work as a means of clearing the whole list, then your procrastination has been beneficial, since look how much you accomplished today.

A task may keep reappearing on a to-do list until it dies of old age and falls off. Perhaps the assignment wasn't all that essential in the first place. If it was something crucial, such as paying the energy bill, and the power was turned off, this is a negative thing. However, occasionally individuals may make a hasty choice to do something and then delay implementing it. After a few days of procrastination, they realize they didn't want to do it in the first place.

Consider the decision to dispose of all of the things of a dead relative. You may plan to get rid of their possessions in a fit of rage because they left you, but after a few days of procrastination, you realize you aren't ready to do it just yet. You would probably be feeling a lot worse if you hadn't procrastinated and gotten rid of everything.

Procrastination may reveal what is and is not essential to you. Nobody puts off doing something they like, such as playing video games or learning a new song on the piano.

So, if the work at hand is constantly pushed aside in favor of anything else, consider if it is really necessary to do so. It may not be, in which case procrastination is beneficial.

When confronted with a huge undertaking, such as a multifaceted project at work or an essential term paper, people often delay. Procrastinating, in this scenario, is a positive thing since it allows time to think about the project and maybe come up with more innovative ideas for finishing it, as well as more inventive methods to achieve it. Procrastination would be regarded as beneficial in this scenario since it provided time for positive thinking.

When human intuition clashes with human rationality, procrastination may be beneficial since it prevents the individual from committing to something they don't want to accomplish. It is all too simple to agree to something on the spur of the moment that you will later regret. Sometimes procrastination is your intuition telling you that you're in a dangerous circumstance.

Chapter 1
Procrastination Causes

Now that you understand how damaging and counterproductive procrastination is, it's time to figure out what causes it. You are now aware of the benefits of avoiding these causes. The reasons for procrastination are many, ranging from previous failures to quick satisfaction. This is why many individuals become victims of apparently innocuous events. No one has ever found a procrastinator attractive since inefficiency and sloth are both unattractive in so many ways.

Mistakes in the Past

You may have been a hardworking person in the past. You never missed a deadline and gave it your best every time. Everything changed, though, when that new boss or supervisor arrived. For him, your finest isn't good enough. He is never happy or satisfied, no matter how hard you try. The same is true for your unappreciative family members. They felt you were lethargic and useless even though you took

out the garbage as soon as it was full and cleaned the vehicle at least twice a week.

These previous experiences have sapped your energy and determination to perform your best and complete the project days or weeks before the deadline.

Of course, the people around you have a role, but you are ultimately accountable for your ideas and actions. Your history should not determine who you are now. Rather, it should serve as a reminder of what you still need to do in the present. You're not putting out your best effort only to be validated by others around you. You're giving it your all so you can boast proudly that you put your all into completing a job. Your superiors will recognize your value in the future.

You just must be efficient, zealous, and accountable constantly.

No one has ever criticized someone for trying his or her best all of the time, right?

Depression

Procrastination may be exacerbated by intense despair.

You wouldn't be able to work on anything if you were in the thick of grief, right? However, if you try it, the results will most certainly be below average. You can't do your chores before the deadline, no matter how

hard you try. Sadness binds you, stopping you from thinking, rationally, and quietly. This specific reason for procrastination is extremely unusual in that it contains multiple components, making it a difficult nut to crack.

You don't just recover from depression. It's a mental illness that can only be treated with persistent and thoughtful support, encouragement, and affirmation. Those around you should be steady and dependable pillars of support, urging you to continue working on something and live despite the terrible sentiments you're now experiencing. Depression has a wide range of reasons, so it's important to devote time to determine what's causing it. Procrastination generally stops after the depression is treated.

Failure apprehension and low self-esteem
Some individuals are just terrified of failing or being ridiculed by others, particularly those whose views they value. They may not have received any severe negative criticism in the past, yet they lack the courage to take even one step ahead.

Their anxieties, though, have origins as well. Perhaps they didn't get as much encouragement or advice when they were younger. It's also conceivable that they were forced to work on something on their own and missed the deadline as a result.

Essentially, they lack a strong basis from which to establish a feeling of responsibility.

They believe they are inept, but the truth is that they are just terrified of failure. They are preoccupied with the negative consequences of their ideas and behaviors, rather than the favorable ones. Although both are equally feasible, they have chosen to focus on what may go wrong. Individuals like this must be reminded that they can do great things, but they must take the first step. They must decide to proceed since the task or project will not be completed on its own. There is always a purpose to progress. Believing in yourself is one of the first stages in completing what has to be done.

Immediate gratification

Many distractions may have an immediate and long-term impact on an individual's productivity. Many sources have become available as technology has advanced.

Various forms of entertainment have also sprouted up. These items make life more joyful and less stressful in many ways. Unfortunately, they may also lead to procrastination in a person's life. Nobody is immune to the powerful influences of television, computer games, talking, and social networking. People did not have anything to do years ago but accomplish their tasks. People now have a plethora of illogical reasons to put things off until the very last minute.

You have a history or marketing report due on Monday, but you opted to spend the weekend watching movies from Friday evening through Sunday afternoon. What do you wind up getting as a result of this? You're under a lot of stress and strain since you're certain you won't be able to complete any of the reports. You may be able to pull an all-nighter, but the stress and rushed nature of the process will only degrade the quality of your work. You fall back on the adage, "It's better to have anything than nothing at all." You must submit something or you will undoubtedly fail.

Laziness

Some folks are just too indolent to accomplish anything at all. They put things off because they don't like their bosses, coworkers, students, or instructors. Their reasoning is straightforward: "I simply don't feel like doing anything." This is difficult to modify since nothing will be done if the individual is hesitant to do anything. You can only push someone so far before he decides to do something about his life. If procrastination is his "thing," it will take some time for him to become responsible.

Yes, laziness can be overcome. It is not fatal, but it is a significant impediment. If you're not in the mood, you won't even contemplate beginning, much alone continuing, your work. However, laziness is infectious. If your teammates or classmates are feeling sluggish, you'll probably go with the flow. Because no one else is moving or doing anything, you will as well. You believe that if they can — and are willing to — cope with the repercussions of procrastination, so can you. Unfortunately, most individuals are ignorant that they have a lot to lose when they spend their time. Furthermore, if you choose to leave anything incomplete, your creativity will suffer. Your thoughts are rendered ineffective because your body refuses to move.

Chapter 2
Organizational Characteristics

Developing the proper traits might help you become more organized.

Ten characteristics are shared by persons who effectively manage their time.

You may be wondering why some individuals seem to be more organized in their life than others. They always appear to be able to do all of their responsibilities quickly and yet have time to assist with other things. This chapter will go over some of the characteristics that all organized individuals have in common.

- They understand what is vital in life—you must realize that not everything you do, no matter what your mind tells you, is significant. Extremely productive people can differentiate between significant and unimportant jobs. They will not get bogged down with little busy work and will reserve it for later when they have completed some of the other major initiatives that they must do.

- They can organize their day—these folks can sit down the night before and identify what tasks they need to do. This helps them to strike the ground running the next morning instead of fumbling about trying to find out what everything has to be done.

- They can get back on track quickly—even if they are interrupted and things aren't going as well as they would want, productive individuals can get back on track and complete all of their responsibilities on time.

- They understand their priorities—for one thing, folks who are productive understand where they want things to go. They are not only capable of doing tasks, but also of completing them properly. They appreciate prioritization, which means they can set their objectives, and these goals will dictate their actions. These productive individuals can say no while maintaining appropriate limits. You are in command of your calendar, so they may create time for other vital activities since they understand that they cannot be accessible for everything.

- They can problem solve—those who are highly productive can react to obstacles, issues, and hurdles with a problem-solving mindset. Those that are unproductive will blame and humiliate themselves into being productive, which will exacerbate the situation. An excellent technique is to watch what is going on and then locate the remedy that you need so that you can have everything fixed up.

- Equip yourself with the necessary tools—some individuals will wait till they have accomplished a decent objective to acquire what they desire. Productive individuals will begin with all of the necessary workspace and resources, rather than waiting for them afterward. If you want to be more productive, make sure you have the necessary tools available from the start so that you can get everything done right away.

- They have the best concentration—it is hard to get things done in life if you do not have a strong focus; you will not be able to do anything. Productive individuals can filter out extraneous distractions while focusing on the work at hand. Fortunately, with a little effort, you will be able to learn how to execute this ability.

- They are organized—you will never be able to get anything done in your life if you are not able to become organized. Very productive people may plan their life. They may store items in a spot where they can find them later so that they don't waste time seeking what they need. They know precisely where these items are, so they can locate them and go right to work.

- They are disciplined—those that are well organized will be among the most disciplined persons you will ever encounter.

  - Highly productive individuals may discover methods to eliminate time wasters, accept personal responsibility, and always try to improve themselves. Essentially, these individuals can hold themselves responsible for the activities that they do for things to be done.

  - They are continuously learning—learning is not something you should stop doing when you finish school; it is something you should do for the rest of your life. Those that are deemed to be highly organized and productive will recognize this and will continue to learn. If they don't know the solution to anything, the highly productive individuals will be able to take on the task of figuring it out. They acquire the necessary skills and training when they lack the ability, and they will work hard to make things happen the way they want them to.

As you can see, there are true qualities seen in persons who are adept at managing their time. If you want to understand how to utilize time management in the most effective method for your requirements, you must first learn how to acquire some of these abilities. Overall, it will assist you in determining how to employ time management to assist you in making things in your life work out better.

Chapter 3
Procrastination-Related Issues

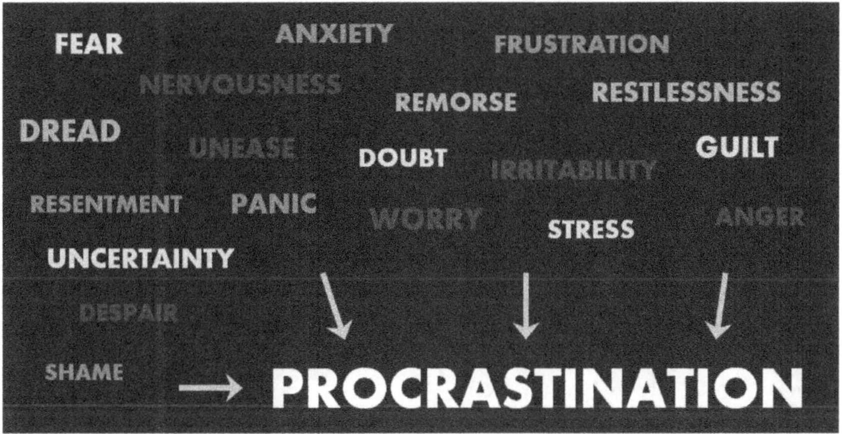

We are all too aware of procrastination at this point. Nobody can claim that they are unaware of procrastination since everyone is aware of it and has experienced it at some time. Some individuals recognize the issue of procrastination and finally address it. Others, however, do not! They need assistance and suggestions to overcome procrastination, which is not anything to be embarrassed about. It is OK to seek assistance and direction. Those who are late in identifying procrastination, on the other hand, experience a slew of issues as a result of procrastination. If you believe you are delaying, take the required actions to rectify the situation. It is harmful to wait until the last minute to treat it. However, let us go through some of the primary issues associated with procrastination. Let's get started:

Wasting valuable time

If you've seen Jay Shetty's motivating films, you'll understand how valuable time is! We spend time as if it has no worth, although it is the most precious resource on the planet. You will not feel good about yourself if you think about the time you squandered. The saddest thing is realizing you've

grown up so much yet haven't changed or improved in the least. You're still standing in the same spot. When this strikes you strongly, you won't be able to move and will become immobile wherever you are! I realize that that might be one of the most dreadful experiences. You may have regrets, but you cannot undo what you have done.

But it's all right, and it's never too late. You may begin right now. You may alter it right now! Consider the modifications that must be implemented and stick to them!

Ignoring opportunity

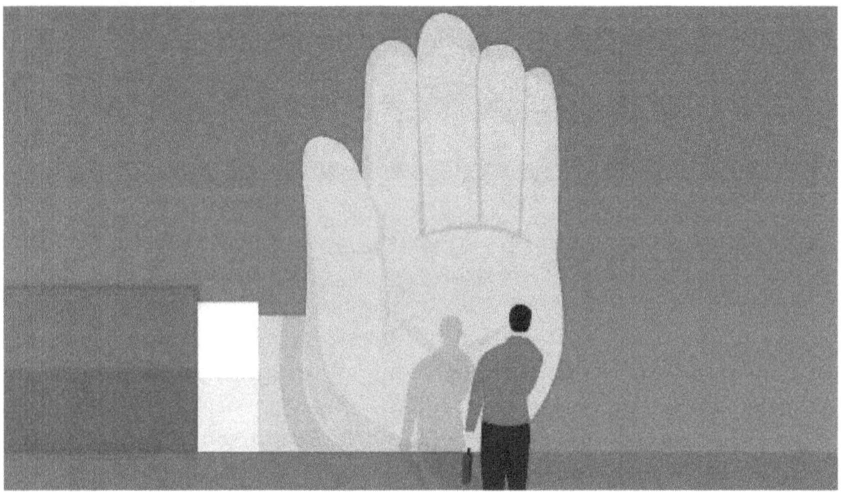

You may have been presented with several possibilities, but you chose to postpone them till tomorrow. Tomorrow is the most often used term among procrastinators. But they have no idea how much devastation it is bringing. When you realize how many amazing possibilities you have passed up, you may want to smack yourself as hard as you can.

But what's the purpose of it?
Remember that opportunities are still coming your way. Yes, you can change, so make use of it!

Failure to achieve objectives
This is going to smack you in the face; consider how long you've been failing to meet your objectives. You may have had a tremendous urge to attain your objectives, but then procrastination set in. You could experience a deep-cut ache in your chest right now if you think about it. However, you may still

fulfill your objectives. You only need to identify and eliminate the causes of procrastination.

Missing the only job

You may not have lost your job, but others have lost their jobs as a result of procrastination. Perhaps procrastination is a quality that companies do not want to see in their workers since it will jeopardize the company's success. Missing deadlines and failing to attend meetings regularly is not a good thing! You should not procrastinate, whether it is at work or home.

Self-esteem decline

Low self-esteem might be one of the causes of procrastination. The unfortunate aspect is that when you put off employment, your self-esteem suffers even more. You begin to doubt your talents. You will also lose confidence in yourself and become vulnerable. Low self-esteem is a danger to your life, therefore research ways to overcome it.

Ineffective decision-making

When you master procrastination, you become a beginner when it comes to decision-making. When you procrastinate, your decisions will be based on what you believe to be correct. At this moment, your emotions will take a toll on you. Poor decision-making will eventually ruin your life.

Reputational harm

It's acceptable if you don't do something you haven't promised. However, saying something you will never do is risky. For example, if you continuously miss deadlines and make excuses, how far can you stretch this lie? Do you believe you'll keep your job after missing so many deadlines? No, I don't believe so.

Your reputation may suffer as a result of the client's negative perception of you. As a result of your procrastination, you are also harming your reputation.

People will cease assigning you jobs or contacting you for essential work since they realize you are not a suitable person. You will always be seen as someone who will be unable to accomplish a job in a reasonable amount of time. You don't believe that a tarnished image is simple to deal with.

Putting your health at risk

Another typical concern related to procrastination is stress, worry, anxiety, and a variety of other health difficulties. If you believe that health difficulties associated with procrastination just affect your mental health, I'm sorry to inform you that there's more to it. Even though mental health concerns are serious, postponing will harm 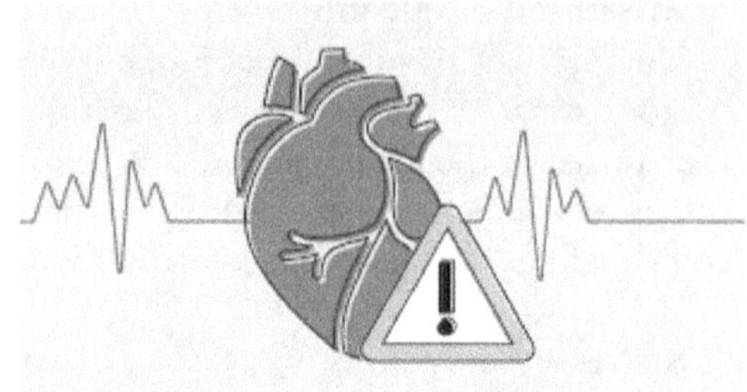 your entire health. As previously indicated, if you do not work properly, you are at risk of contracting several ailments. Procrastination causes you to work all hours of the day and night without giving your body any attention. Do you realize how fragile your body is? Do you know how to manage your body with care? You wouldn't even consider procrastinating if you knew all of this. Procrastinators, on the whole, don't spend much time evaluating these topics. Instead, they go about their business - squandering time!

You are sacrificing your happiness.

You won't comprehend the importance of sacrificing happiness until it strikes you severely. You may often procrastinate, but you complete your task in a matter of minutes, which leads you to believe that you are capable of completing anything when you want to do it. There is a distinct distinction between determination and procrastination.

Determination is shown when you do not postpone the task for the second time.

Basically, by doing the task at the last minute, you are wasting a lot of time. For example, if a family function is scheduled, you will be unable to attend since you are too busy working.

Similarly, when you postpone, you may forfeit your enjoyment. Procrastination is not only bad for your health, but it also makes you sad!

These are only a few of the most prevalent difficulties associated with procrastination, but there are many more serious issues. You are fortunate in that you have resolved to change, which is why you have reached the last page of this book. I hope you make a positive transformation and live a fruitful life!

Chapter 4
Motivation – More Than Just a Feeling?

Where Many People Begin

Many individuals, when asked how to avoid procrastination, would turn to motivation to assist them to break the vicious cycle.

This is because most people believe that motivation is what drives the behavior in the first place. Consider it a three-way process:

Positive emotional state => action => ideas (motivation)

A person who wants to become in shape at the gym may plaster their walls and refrigerator with images of fit individuals for motivation's sake.

Someone who wants to thrive in business may benefit from listening to a motivating speech on self-confidence and accomplishment.

Intuitively, this seems to be a decent place to start. There are even lecturers and authors whose professions are devoted to encouraging us in the contemporary world. It is a profitable company. However, it is based on a falsehood or at least a half-truth. Motivation by itself achieves nothing. Why?

Here's an example to demonstrate and investigate why motivation isn't a panacea for procrastination. Assume you wish to drop 10 pounds after seeing the scale steadily creeping up on you. You then motivate yourself to act. "Today is the day I start reducing calories," you tell yourself. "I'm going to do it this time." You remember how amazing it felt the last time you were physically fit, and you vow to yourself that the memory of this joyful achievement will carry you over the finish line.

Each morning, you begin to hype yourself up, telling yourself, 'I am going to stick to my diet today.' You read inspiring blogs on the topic. This will keep you on track with your diet for a while. You see minor successes on the scale, which delights you and renews your enthusiasm. However, one day at work, you get a scolding from your manager. Your mood plummets, so you decide to self-medicate with cookies and a Netflix marathon. This makes you feel awful about staying on your diet, so you ask yourself, 'Why to bother?' I've already screwed everything up, so there's no sense in even trying.' When your motivation wanes, the diet is done.

The Negative Mind and Procrastination

Being negative is usually the easy choice; being positive requires a lot more work. A negative mindset will just add to your reasons to procrastinate since you'll always find a hundred excuses not to do anything, even if you have one solid reason why you should.

You will never find the additional push and motivation you need to break the pattern of procrastination if you don't give yourself enough credit and trust in yourself enough. A negative mentality might lead you to believe that you're not good enough or worthy enough and that it would be better to simply not do anything at all rather than attempt and risk failure.

Why Doesn't Motivation Work?

Why is it that motivation does not help to overcome procrastination? Simple.

Motivation is founded on human emotions, and human emotions, like humans, are extremely malleable and vulnerable to a variety of external stimuli. Motivation is not a solid foundation upon which to construct your home. It's more like sand on a beach, shifting with the tides.

This is why the gym is so packed in January, but it will be back to normal by mid-February. The emotional high of a New Year's resolve propels people on. 'It's a new year, and I'm going to be a new me,' they tell themselves. They are pleased with their determination, and their short-term successes motivate them for about a month. Then there's life. The "high" of the New Year disappears, as do the good sentiments that carried them along. When the emotional flood recedes, so does their capacity to persevere in the gym.

Laziness is a motivational stumbling block.

Just as motivation propels us forward, a lack of drive (demotivation) propels us downward. To put it another way, it drives us to become lazy.

You are particularly vulnerable to this hazard if you accept the illusion that you must be motivated to act. This is because laziness is just a lack of drive that has become habitual. Let's return to the diet example and the downward spiral of demotivation to better comprehend this phenomenon. The demotivation spiral occurs when an emotional crisis deprives us of our sense of motivation. Your boss screams at you, interrupting your emotional high from diet success. You eat to soothe yourself when your drive wanes. Then you feel bad about cheating, and your drive vanishes.

You begin to believe that "if I fail at my diet once, it's not such a huge thing."

However, someone who relies on motivation may become fatalistic in their thinking after a few of these unavoidable downhill spirals. "Why should I even attempt to diet?" they may ask themselves. "It never works." "I'm constantly failing." Their self-esteem has suffered. This person's lack of motivation has become habitual.

In other words, waiting for inspiration causes us to become inactive and lethargic.

This results in boredom, despair, and a poor sense of self-esteem. Motivation, with its links to our emotions, never appears in such a situation. This creates a loop in which we wait for inspiration, but none occurs, and hence we do not act. Inaction makes us feel horrible about our sloth, and these negative sentiments make it much more difficult to conjure motivation. We have developed a habit of passivity and lethargy.

Laziness is known by many different names. Some call it idleness, while others name it slothfulness, indolence, lethargy, and a variety of other terms. It is a highly hazardous habit to have since it may rapidly become a behavioral pattern if done often enough. The problem with laziness is that it silently sneaks in and takes hold of you, and you won't even recognize it until it's too late, and breaking out of that pattern of behavior becomes difficult. It is a vice that takes over without your knowledge, which is what makes it hazardous.

This is why you succumb to procrastination more often than you would want.

It always begins innocently enough, with you indulging in a few lazy days because you believe you have earned this much-needed rest. A person who acts only when they feel like it (or, in other words, only when they are motivated) gradually develops the habit of being lethargic. Only when you feel like doing something well do you do it. You wouldn't bother if you didn't. Because being lazy, resting, and doing nothing feels so nice, you eventually start doing more of it. You gradually begin to submit to the concept and give in to your wants each time you don't want to do anything until this habit becomes a part of your lifestyle over time. It may seem innocuous enough, but eliminating laziness once it has firmly taken hold is not as simple as it appears.

Motivation comes after action.

Ask yourself, "Do I feel inspired to write a 30-page paper when I stare at a blank computer screen?"

Do I want to learn a new language when I can barely say 'oui' and 'non'?
In the first 100 meters, do I feel like jogging 100 miles to warm up my frigid muscles?

You most certainly replied 'no' to the preceding questions. In the case of the paper, the writer feels more at ease and competent after doing research and writing a few lines. This is when he starts to feel motivated about a project.

As she learns a few more words and successfully strings together a few sentences, the language learner feels motivated.

With each mile that passes, the runner's drive grows.

Another peculiarity of motivation is that it often follows. Small triumphs, such as the language student saying a few sentences or the runner putting a few kilometers behind him, ignite drive when action is done.

As the writer learns more about the topic, she gets confidence and drives. This is the proper three-way procedure:

Positive emotional state => motivation => action

The Rightful Place of Motivation

Is motivation, therefore, a negative thing? Not. Motivation may either get you started correctly or come up after you've already started acting. It may also help you achieve shorter-term objectives. We can utilize motivation to our advantage if we grasp how it works.

To master motivation, we must keep in mind that it is dependent on our emotions. We may use pleasant emotional states or external incentive elements to get started on modest initiatives. The pleasant feelings associated with making a New Year's resolution may be enough to get us started at the gym if we turn to additional tactics to keep us on track. The prospect of your in-laws' impending visit may be enough to motivate you to clear out the shoe closet.

We might also recall that motivation is sometimes late to the party. We may remind ourselves that even though we don't feel inspired right now, we could receive a much-needed boost once we get started.

Motivation, on the other hand, is an untrustworthy companion. At worst, it's a deception that may imprison us in a cycle of lethargy and inactivity. For the long term, we need something more reliable, something that is there even when inspiration is lacking.

When individuals recognize what occurs when motivation fails because it is beyond their control, they shift their focus to something they know they can manage — willpower. Willpower is defined as "energetic resolve" by Merriam Webster.

Willpower is what motivates us to get out of bed in the morning and go to work, even if it is not where we want to be. Nobody likes to spend 8 hours of their day cooped up in a cubicle performing a job they don't enjoy, but they do it anyway because they have to.

A Closer Look at Will Power

According to science, the prefrontal cortex is a specialized portion of our brain that regulates our decision-making, our capacity to plan for the future

and make decisions that will benefit us in the long term. This portion of the brain is placed behind the eyes in front of the skull. Researchers have mapped the brains of people with strong and weak willpower and discovered changes in activity in this region of the brain.

This little area of the brain might be referred to as the 'willpower muscle.' And it works in the same manner as your other muscles: if you don't utilize it, you lose it! The good news is that it can be repaired, retrained, and strengthened just like a muscle.

Training the Willpower Muscle - Begin Small and Work Your Way Up

If willpower is a muscle, the only way to build it is to exercise it over time. We may gradually increase our willpower by taking little measures against our natural tendencies. If you're having trouble writing academic papers, you may start simple. Regardless of how you feel, practice writing one page at a time. Then it was two pages, then three.

If you have trouble choosing good eating choices, you may start with one nutritious meal a day and work your way up to two, then three. You get the picture. As you hone your willpower on these tiny activities, it will become strong enough to take on larger and more complicated obstacles.

If you're not sure where to start growing your willpower muscle, or if you recognize you have an inherently weak willpower, taking up a sport or going to the gym is a fantastic place to start. The mind/body link is very potent, and exercising both simultaneously may have a synergistic impact. If you start at the gym by walking a half-mile, a mile, then jogging for a few minutes, then running a 5 k, you will see a difference in both your physical strength and the strength of your willpower.

Remember the saying, "A thousand miles begin with a single step." Consider things that you often struggle with and divide them into smaller parts. Exercising your willpower muscles by completing one tiny portion of a job is a good way to start. As previously said, inspiration will often follow these modest steps to action and assist you in moving forward.

Is Willpower the Answer?

Willpower seems to be the final answer to our procrastination issue. You can train it, and unlike your emotions, you can manage it, thus there's no negative, right? Consider the following scenario:

Your alarm clock goes off in the morning. "Just 5 more minutes of sleep," your brain urges. "I MUST get up and go to work," you say, flexing your determination. I AM GOING TO DO IT." You drag yourself out of bed and go to have breakfast, where you are presented with an option.

Oatmeal or pastry? Once again, you must force yourself to make the healthier option. "I HAVE TO EAT BETTER," I told myself I'd do it. Don't even consider it, chocolate donut!" You devour the porridge, hating every mouthful. You've already had two willpower fights in the first 10 minutes of your day. It's going to be an exhausting day.

Even just envisioning this situation is exhausting. There is a reason behind this. Going against our natural impulses and using our willpower requires a lot of work. In the past decade or two, scientists have begun to investigate willpower and the notion that willpower is a finite resource. Willpower depletion is a concept being researched by scientists.

In 1996, psychologist Roy Baumeister performed research dubbed the Chocolate-and-Radish Experience to explore the idea of willpower. Baumeister attracted a group of test volunteers with the aroma of freshly baked cookies in this experiment. They were then escorted into a room where they were presented with a plate of cookies and a bowl of radishes. Some individuals were instructed to consume the radishes, while others were permitted to eat cookies. Following that, both groups were given a challenging geometry task to tackle. The radishes group gave up on the arithmetic task twice as quickly as the cookie group. The researchers determined that those who ate radishes reduced their stores of willpower in rejecting the cookie fragrance. They just had less willpower than the group that got to eat cookies when they tackled the arithmetic assignment.

The fundamental issue with attempting to utilize willpower to win the procrastination war is that if you spend your whole life battling against your procrastination inclinations, just like in a real battle, you will eventually wear out and be tired. As a result, extremely few individuals succeed in overcoming procrastination only by willpower.

Good for sprinting but not for running the marathon.

The good news is that we can strengthen our willpower via deliberate exercise. The bad news is that no matter how hard we train, we will always have a limited quantity of willpower and may be unable to manage when we run out of "gas." However, if our willpower wanes, we will revert to our old procrastinating patterns. Nonetheless, willpower is an important aspect of the picture. Willpower will bring you to the finish line in the last mile of a marathon. But what will motivate you to complete the first twenty-five miles?

Chapter 5
Build the Intention to Break Procrastination

Every path towards a goal starts with a commitment; a commitment to developing, having greater control of your nerves and working with passion and endurance towards the final objective to eventually realize it.

You are unlikely to make consistent progress toward a goal unless you have a strong commitment and a clear purpose to do so. This is why your quest to overcome procrastination must begin with a firm commitment.

Accept Your Issue

To have a clear goal to tackle your issue, you must first accept that you have a problem to address. You will not completely understand the consequences of your situation until you admit it, and you will not strive diligently to solve it unless you acknowledge it. Accepting your issue gets simpler when you concentrate on how it affects (read: sabotages) your life. To do this, complete the following steps:

- Examine your daily routine from the moment you get up until you go to bed, and make a list of all the chores you do.

- Make a note of how much time you dedicate to each assignment.

- Evaluate the value of each activity on the list and consider what it helped you accomplish that day. For example, if you spent 3 hours studying your final year philosophy project in college, what result did you obtain as a result of your research? Were you able to do relevant research, or were you dissatisfied with your results since you did not commit three full hours to investigate the topic? Consider whether or not every work you do daily contributes to the achievement of anything worthwhile in the long run. Are you able to get $100 if your aim for the day is to earn $100? And to accomplish it in light of the time you spend on work-related tasks?

- Consider how much time you spend on the items on the list and how much of that time is spent on other activities. Consider what you accomplished in those two hours if you spent two hours writing a 200-word email to a possible investor in your company. Were you thinking about the content?

Did you spend 1.5 hours utilizing the email and researching it to guarantee you created a well-structured and successful email?

Do you spend 30 minutes on social media on your phone and just 30 minutes on the real task? The devil is always in the details, or this instance, in the minutes. Consider the chores you want to do daily but fail to complete. Write those things down and compare their relevance and the objectives they would have helped you attain with the ones currently on your list. Why do you think that happened if you had planned to write a blog post for your blog, email some PR firms, pitch a proposal to a potential client, do some household chores like laundry and dinner preparation, and had to spend 2 hours with your family, but you only ended up writing a blog post and doing laundry? What went wrong, and where did it go wrong, that caused you to sabotage your whole strategy and fail to meet your daily goals?

Once you've written out all of the answers to the questions and assessed your routine, read through the account a few times and you'll understand how prone you are to procrastination and how destructive it is for you within minutes. When you compare the results you achieve daily to the desired outcomes, you will immediately realize how your habit of deferring important tasks and engaging in something less meaningful but more appealing while working on an important task is a poisonous habit that is only destroying your life. This insight will assist you in accepting your predicament.

It is critical to make a verbal and then a handwritten proclamation of assent to put things in writing. "I have a horrible tendency of procrastinating critical things, and I am going to work hard to overcome this behavior," say and write down. Your proclamation may alter, but the gist should remain the same.

Make a Firm Commitment Supported by compelling Whys

Now that you've identified your issue and committed to resolving it, you need to consolidate and deepen your resolve by tying it to a convincing why. You must have a compelling reason, or perhaps numerous reasons, why you must overcome your poor habit of procrastination to work diligently toward your objective.

Because they are the reasons why you are seeking that goal, the whys linked with each objective encourage you to strive towards its realization. Why would you ever want to interrupt the cycle of procrastination if there is no motive to do so? Why would you go to the gym or concentrate on healthy food if losing weight isn't essential to you? To combat procrastination, you must first determine why you want to accomplish it.

Close your eyes, or leave them open if you like, and consider the most pressing problem in your life right now. It might be anything that makes you unhappy, causes you pain, or prevents you from living a perfectly fulfilled and joyful life. It might be your fight to lose weight, the difficulties you are having in starting your company, your battle with depression and the desire to succumb to it, or anything else that is significantly causing friction in your life and preventing you from enjoying the life you truly want.

Write down your findings, and when you recollect your work routine and how much time you spend on really significant chores against those that just waste your time, you will see that procrastination is a big reason you are failing to attain your intended objectives. Consider how your life might improve if this happened.

If you gathered the fortitude to resist your temptations and overcome procrastination to conduct genuine work. Write those reasons down and use them to fuel your determination to follow through on your pledge to fight procrastination.

Set a Specific Goal

Set a very specific objective to truly fight this terrible habit now that you have a deeper knowledge of why you need to overcome your inclination to delay and are more motivated than ever to work towards this particular goal. You might have various objectives on your list that you want to achieve to live a more meaningful, happy life, but it is tough to work on several goals at the same time.

Remember that you only have a limited quantity of willpower to work on a certain activity, and that willpower depletes with each step you take toward a specific objective. As a result, if you work for three hours straight on constructing your company's website, you will most likely be weary and unable to focus on another high-priority objective for a couple of hours.

Slow and steady is the best way to guarantee you don't run out of willpower to work on anything significant. Make a list of the objectives you want to focus on to become more active, energetic, and productive, but choose one key one from the list to concentrate on first.

Make your objective as precise and explicit as possible so you know exactly what you're aiming for. If you want to increase your income, consider how much you would want to make each month and compare it to how much you receive. If you put off cleaning your home, consider how clean you want it to be and set a precise goal based on that. Write down your aim in your notebook after you have a better understanding of it.

You now have a compelling cause to conquer your procrastination.

Next, you must devise an action plan to work tirelessly toward this objective while resisting every temptation that arises.

Chapter 6
Making Quick Decisions

Making a quick choice is one of the most effective techniques to overcome procrastination. You must be quick to make judgments and slow to change them. Finishers realized a long time ago that you can't go ahead if you can't execute a choice as quickly as feasible.

You can't progress from one stage of life to another if you can't make quick judgments. You must grasp the skill of quick decision-making if you want to lessen your chances of losing out on possibilities.

Things to think about before making a quick decision:

Reduce your alternatives.

Naturally, when we have too many alternatives, we tend to think about them for a long period and, as a consequence, make delayed decisions. Even if you have all of your alternatives, it is critical to have a restricted set of possibilities. Make time for research and another for execution to limit the quantity of information you ingest.

There are always fresh possibilities, new ideas, and different approaches to accomplishing the same goal. However, you should choose fewer methodologists so that you do not overburden yourself with possibilities.

Distinguish between excellent and poor options.

You must make both excellent and terrible decisions in business and education. You should be able to learn from your errors and constantly look for the positive aspects of any negative event. Regardless of the dangers involved, make quicker judgments to investigate things.

When you remain in your cage and never expose yourself to new situations, it's difficult to tell what's good and what's terrible. Bad decisions may be characterized by the consequence or the stress you must endure implementing a certain solution.

Pay attention to your inner instinct.

It is also critical to follow your intuition to make the right option. Your emotions and instincts are imprinted by your prior experiences. You don't always require complete knowledge regarding the legitimacy of your choices. Simply follow your instincts and make judgments depending on whether you receive a favorable or bad feeling from a certain individual. You may always test the usefulness of your gut instinct by putting your options to the test. Once you have gained trust, you may go further in matching your choices with the larger aim.

Keep in mind the repercussions of indecision.

When you have too many options, remind yourself of the repercussions of indecision. These implications include a delay in success, the loss of precious chances, a lack of experiences, and slowness in gaining true influence over the things around you.

When you can realize the effects that are most relevant to your person or business partner, you will be forced to make quick selections. People who make quick judgments are frequently slow to change their minds. They often have adequate time to investigate every aspect of the precise selection they've made. As a result, they don't have to be concerned about a shortage of real-time to do tasks quickly.

Align your time and your money.

Begin to consider your time as money. If you are an entrepreneur, you will grasp the value of time and money in accomplishing higher objectives You don't have to be generating money directly with your time to grasp this, but you should be able to examine the amount of time required to do a certain activity, how much you are paid every month, and divide the amount by the number of workdays. Normally, you should be able to set up a certain amount of time for each work, so your decision-making will be quick to validate your efficiency.

Consider the expansion.

Decisiveness is a life-changing step. You cannot just decide to be determined when you get up in the morning. Making a decision is an art, a skill set that must be acquired and practiced. Never underestimate the importance of making a quick choice on a basic problem.

Once you've mastered easy decision-making and reduced the habit of reflection, you'll be able to effortlessly concentrate on what matters and make the appropriate decisions without the need for true motivation. Allow your decision-making to become natural, and you will not have to regret making a poor choice. Making a quick choice should provide you the opportunity to find something greater and better than what you now have.

Learn from the Pros

Leaders make distinct choices, which is why they are successful in their pursuits. As a leader, you must be able to make quick decisions to keep your people's hopes alive.

The principle of convenience

Being a leader entails having at least one person for whom you are accountable. Traditionally, we are constantly accountable for someone, whether at work or school. The law of convenience requires you to delegate authority over certain aspects of your leadership.

Instead of being concerned about making an uncertain judgment, delegate decision-making authority to trustworthy team members so that you can evaluate their capacity to make tough distinctions. You can easily save time with them, and you may increase their confidence without shattering yours. It is beneficial for a leader to take a vacation from the burden of decision-making.

In the business world, having a strong management team is critical, and enabling your trustees to make your decisions automatically gives them the experiences they need for better management of your organization. Furthermore, new ideas and methodologies might be simply implemented.

Instead of displaying authority in decision-making, the leader implements a voting mechanism that allows everyone to participate in decision-making. In this instance, majorities always win, and everyone on the team will suffer the repercussions of poor decision-making.

It is an excellent technique to bring people together and ensure that every decision is affected by the majority of team members. When there are two options on the table, the final vote may be done to decide which is the best.

Although the effectiveness of this kind of decision-making is debatable, it is the most efficient technique to save time in many ways.

Making decisions in collaboration

To make a final choice in a company or institution, insight and input from team members are essential. Other leaders or team members will be asked to provide comments to the leader. Even though the leader is supposed to make the ultimate choice, his decision is constantly influenced by the facts gathered from other members' input.

Only evidence gathered from other team members is utilized to make a long-term decision. Leaders often avoid those who completely agree with them and instead resort to constructive criticism on the effectiveness of their current and previous decisions.

Surround yourself with individuals who are knowledgeable and capable of debating your decision-making abilities. This is necessary to purify your information and to have the finest method to make final decisions. Your choice must be genuine. This is the only way to ensure that you are making the best selection possible.

The command strategy

This strategy is often used when leaders have much more expertise than the rest of their team. There is no time to dither over the veracity of your selections in this circumstance. You just make the choice and insist that your whole staff adhere to it with zeal and consistency. If anything goes wrong, you may be accused, but you must still find a way out to find a permanent solution.

Most individuals who are obliged to make such selections always turn out to be better at making tough decisions, especially when faced with a plethora of enticing options. At some point, the number of options you have will be less important than your ability to make quick judgments. Keep in mind that your staff will always need effective and rapid supervision from you. It is your job to make a quick decision so that you do not undermine their trust by continuing deliberating or asking them which option is preferable.

When others are stressed, you must be confident and strategic, making quick judgments without fear of failure. Always keep in mind the amount of time remaining to make final judgments as well as the deadlines involved. To make an excellent final choice, the hazards of delay must also be considered.

Chapter 7
Self-Control

We all avoid performing some tasks from time to time. Really, who wants to clear out the garage? Procrastinators have pushed task avoidance to new heights. They go out of their way to find something else to do rather than accomplishing the work at hand.

Procrastination is a battle between you and your capacity for self-control. It also highlights our inability to anticipate the future, since we constantly expect to do this chore tomorrow, never knowing what tomorrow may bring. Our desires exploit our ambitions, and soon life is just about making ourselves feel good now. Unfortunately, that euphoria is fleeting because, although it may seem nice to put things off today, the practice of procrastination leads to feelings of inadequacy and failure in the long run.

Negative emotions take over, and the procrastinator finally gives up.

Procrastination is heavily reliant on our capacity to deceive ourselves.

We persuade ourselves that it will be completed tomorrow, even when we know it will not. And we are well aware that we are deceiving ourselves.

Furthermore, the world we live in provides us with several possibilities to divert ourselves with activities that are much more engaging than finishing our task or working toward a goal. However, it is possible to stop the habit of procrastination and teach ourselves to complete tasks on time. It requires dedication and hard effort. It's not going to be easy. It may include eliminating some hobbies or people from your life. However, if breaking the negative habit of procrastinating is crucial to you, you will be able to accomplish so.

Remember when the infant was beginning to walk? How did he take his initial cautious steps and begin a new route in his brain, then walk those first few steps to complete the circuit in his brain? Procrastination as a habit has its pathways in the brain, both those that exist due to the structure of the brain and those that we have formed as a result of our persistent procrastination. It will now be required to create new neural pathways to avoid the pathways that lead to automatic procrastination.

Let us begin by noting that, although procrastination may be an entrenched habit, it is also a habit of choice. We decide to postpone. We opt to do something else rather than what we need to do. We choose to do every other activity on our to-do list while deferring the critical duty until the end of the day when there is no more time in the day.

Rather than starting on that term paper, we decide to browse the internet.

We'd rather manufacture excuses for why we can't get everything done than re-evaluate everything we've promised ourselves to complete. Procrastination is a process in which we deliberately choose to engage, and we must now actively choose to replace this bad habit with a good one.

The majority of what we do on any given day is the result of a habit. We get up, go to bed, shower, eat, and drive—all of these behaviors have become routines. If our behaviors aren't benefiting us, they won't help us attain the objectives we set for ourselves. Procrastination is a bad habit that will never get us anywhere in life since it is all about avoiding doing the things we need to accomplish. The inverse of procrastination is doing things we don't want to do because we know we have to.

The first step is to take an honest inventory of your life as it now stands.

If you have no notion where your life is right now, you will have no beginning point from which to transform your life. And procrastination is a part of your life right now. Nobody procrastinates simply at work or at home;

we do it everywhere and all the time. So, accept who you are right now because that is all you have to work with. Be willing to acknowledge where you are in your life right now.

Recognize the truth of your current situation. Admit to all of your half-finished jobs, your horrible habit of procrastination, and all of the occasions you failed to complete a task because you procrastinated. Consider all of the opportunities you've passed up because you prefer to postpone.

Do everything as gently as possible. After all, we're talking about you, a human being, and we're trying to be truthful without being disrespectful. You are not evil; you just have a poor habit. You are not a failure; you just fail to perform things when they are required. You are not sluggish; on the contrary, you are actively engaged in task avoidance.

While it may seem to be a simple workout, it may be one of the most difficult you have ever attempted. It necessitates being completely honest with oneself, which is not always easy. We all project a picture of ourselves, of how we want everyone to view us, to the outside world, which is generally just a tiny portion of who we are. We are the sports star, the brilliant office intern, the faithful daughter, or the terrific best friend who is always accessible. But it is not the whole picture of who we are. Because the sports star has bad days, the skilled intern misspells words in reports, the loyal daughter pretends to be in the bathroom rather than answering the phone when mom calls, and the wonderful best friend sometimes skips dates with her besties.

Make a list of everything in your life that you want to alter.
Make a note of them on paper so you have a record to refer to.

Make a list of everything. Be truthful, since you're doing this to become a better version of yourself in the future. You're attempting to repair yourself, and you can't fix yourself until you know where you're starting from.

Brantley does not complete assignments on time, does not attend all of his courses, and does not prepare for examinations even when he is aware that they are planned.

Amanda has no plan in place to keep the home tidy. She also does not know how to maintain the cleanliness of the home.

Jessie wants to be able to live on her own someday, but she knows her present part-time work will never be enough to support her. She has also considered returning to school, but she has no clue what she might find intriguing enough to go to school for.

George would want to pursue other changes in his professional life, but he is unsure about what he should pursue or even where to begin.

Melanie wishes she had more free time and that she didn't feel like a letdown to everyone in her life.

Ronnie wants to be physically fit. He aspires to appear like one of the bodybuilders shown on the covers of men's fitness magazines.

So, after you've created a written scenario of where you are in life, go through it again. Have you read what you wrote? That person is you. That is the "you" with whom we are now collaborating. Don't worry if you don't like what you see because we'll work hard to make it so you do. You should adore yourself. You should believe you are the most amazing creature on the planet. Stop delaying and start taking care of yourself.

Accept yourself exactly where you are now so that you may begin to repair the you that exists. And be prepared to be brutally honest along the way. You can't remedy something you don't know about or refuse to recognize exists. If you are not willing to view your life as it is, you will not be able to alter it. You must acknowledge what is true so that you may devise a strategy to improve the aspects of your life that you dislike. Accept that you procrastinate and that you want to improve your self-discipline so that your life may be what you want it to be.

Now that you've admitted that your life isn't exactly going the way you want it to and that a change is required, it's time to conduct some introspection to find out why you delay. This portion may be particularly challenging since it will need you to examine what it is about the life that you dislike. We will not use the word 'wrong,' since this is your life, and although it may not be working right now, we will not label it as such. It is preferable to think as optimistically as possible. You have a chance for progress in your life, and you are making use of it.

So, what is the reason behind your procrastination? Ask yourself what causes you to delay, and remember to be honest with yourself since this is all for you.

Do you put off doing tasks for whatever reason you can think of? Are you too busy, weary, or anything to do that task? If this describes you, you are a procrastinating procrastinator.

Are you hooked on generating list after list of things that need to be done but seldom cross anything off the list? Is it difficult to complete work because you get so engrossed in one detail that the deadline passes you by? Then you are a procrastinator who makes lists.

Do you shun new experiences because you are terrified of change? Do you resist taking on new challenges because you believe they would be uncomfortable? Is it simple for you to accomplish nothing because you lack confidence in your abilities? If you recognize yourself here, you are a worrisome procrastinator.

Do you create unreasonable objectives and tasks and then do nothing about them because you believe you will fail anyway? Are you dissatisfied with a work well done because you believe it must be completely flawless or it just isn't good enough? If this describes you, you're a perfectionist procrastinator.

Isn't daydreaming enjoyable? Do you often daydream when you have work to do? Would you prefer to think about nice goods and nice locations than perform real work? You are a procrastinator who daydreams.

Have you ever failed to accomplish a single assignment in your life?

Are you particularly adept at finding something else to do when there are certain tasks to be completed? Is it tough for you to concentrate on just one subject at a time? If it is, you are a procrastinator who is distracted.

Perform you believe you are too talented to do some things? Do you believe it is vital for you to have complete control over every event, including what happens at any given time of day? Do you avoid commencing necessary tasks as a result of this? If you perform any of these things, you are a defiant procrastinator.

Is everyone on your side? Are you accessible to assist everyone in your environment at all hours of the day and night? Do you prioritize your own needs to meet the needs of your friends and family?

Are you unable to assist everyone since there are so many individuals who need your assistance? If you can identify with this, you are a chronic procrastinator.

Are you working till the wee hours of the morning again? Is the very last minute when you start working on an essential project? Are you the kind that waits until everything has reached a crisis point before stepping in to attempt to solve the problem? If this describes you, you are a crisis procrastinator.

Chapter 8
Have SMART to Do Lists

After discussing three broad techniques for overcoming procrastination, we'll go through ten particular measures that can help you maximize your productivity. Personal productivity and not procrastinating are two factors that feed off of each other, and the more they feed off of each other, the more productive and determined you get to get more things done. In this chapter, we'll go through how to make sensible to-do lists.

When you think about it, utilizing a to-do list seems to be as easy as breathing. So, why the need for a whole chapter on the subject?

Believe me, it's not as easy as it seems. To-do lists are not all made equal, and the quality of your to-do lists may have a significant influence on your capacity to maximize personal productivity.

And if you don't build practical and clever to-do lists, it might hurt your productivity. So, what constitutes a good and practical to-do list? A S.M.A.R.T. to-do list is specified, measurable, attainable, realistic, and time-bound.

SPECIFIC

Your to-do list entries must be explicit in terms of what needs to be completed. Otherwise, you'll struggle to be productive.

Why? If the items on your to-do list are ambiguous, such as "get as much work done as possible" or "feel wonderful," you'll run into two potential personal productivity issues. The first is being unable to tell objectively when you have completed your job satisfactorily. What, for example, does "as much labor as possible" imply? Does this imply processing at least one, two, or twenty transactions every day? What exactly does "feeling wonderful" imply?

What do you have to do to feel fantastic? Feeling fantastic isn't even a goal; it's only a byproduct or effect of achieving certain objectives, such as making a major business transaction.

MEASURABLE

This implies that things on your to-do list may be stated numerically or split down into quantifiable components. Why?

The more quantifiable it is, the more objectively you can assess whether or not an item on your to-do list has already been completed. For example, it will be extremely difficult, if not impossible, to objectively determine whether you have successfully "become more joyful" because joy cannot be measured, as opposed to "feed 10 more homeless people today compared to last week" or "feed 20 homeless people this week," both of which can be objectively determined.

ATTAINABLE

Your to-do list, or the tasks on it, should be something that can be done in a reasonable amount of time. Otherwise, you'll be unproductive the majority of the time, which may lead to a downward circle of growing procrastination, unproductivity, and feeling more uninspired to get things done. However, if your to-do list is doable or practical, it will enhance your productivity, morale, and capacity to beat procrastination in the teeth!

Awesome!

Instead of putting things like "achieve world peace" or "sell $1.0 million worth of pop tarts within the week," your to-do list should include things like "schedule a 1-hour meeting between Mr. Smith and Ms. Klein to settle their misunderstanding" or "sell $50 worth of pop tarts tomorrow at the county fair."

The quantity of tasks on your daily to-do list is another aspect of being "realistic." If you are not cautious, it is easy to create a counterproductive daily to-do list, i.e., a discouraging to-do list that may make you unproductive and, ultimately, transform you into a chronic procrastinator. If you overcrowd your daily to-do lists with at least 50 distinct things, you're likely to feel overwhelmed (and procrastinate), unable to complete all of your daily duties, and with an ever-increasing pile of incomplete work! When this occurs frequently, you'll lose motivation to complete your chores, postpone, and finally become considerably less productive. That is why, as a general rule, you should restrict the number of significant jobs you must do for the day to no more than three. Anything more may raise your chances of being overwhelmed and procrastinating greatly.

RELEVANT

A relevant to-do list is focused on assisting you in achieving your life's most essential objectives. In other words, it is not cluttered with chores and ambitions. Furthermore, by concentrating just on chores that are related to your life's greatest or most essential objectives, you unwittingly restrict the number of things to complete daily, assisting you in making your to-do list much more practical or doable.

TIME-BOUND

Finally, each item on your to-do list must have a deadline. Why? If they don't have a deadline, you won't feel compelled to finish them! If you've ever intended to lose 10 pounds but didn't give yourself a time limit or a deadline, the temptation to put it off, i.e., procrastinate, gets much, much greater!

Rather than just stating "complete writing my essay or report," you might be more detailed or time-bound by adding "finish writing my essay or report by noon at the latest." This will give you a stronger feeling of urgency to complete the activity and reach a higher degree of attention. Setting shorter personal deadlines may improve your feeling of urgency to complete your activities, allowing you to concentrate much better on what is vital.

Chapter 9
The Action Priority Matrix

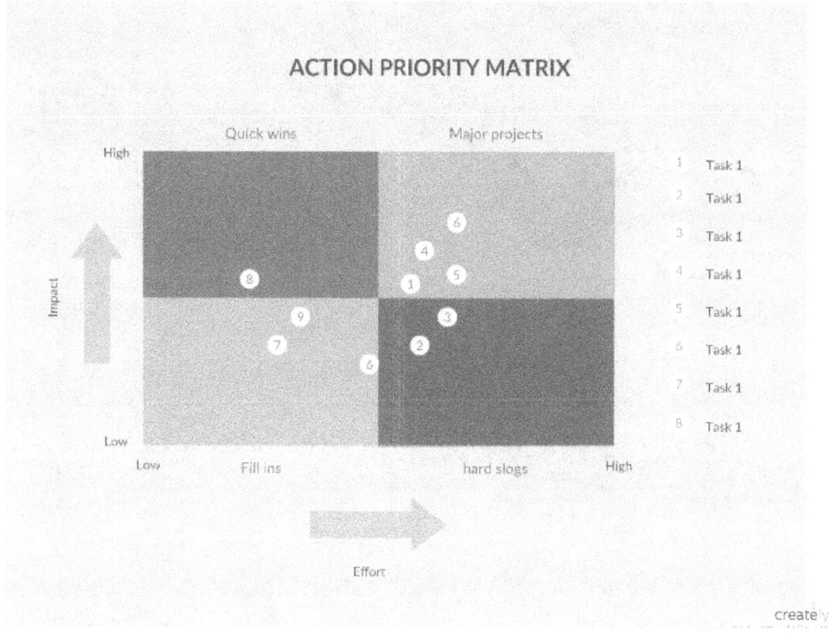

You must learn how to prioritize your workload and time, whether at home or work, to better discern between the urgent and the important.

You may organize your jobs into their proper categories by using a grid, such as the action priority matrix.

As you can see, it is a diagram that may assist you in determining which tasks to prioritize and which to avoid to make the most use of your opportunities, energy, and time.

You can spend more of your time on high-value tasks that keep you going ahead if you utilize an action priority matrix to pick your activities carefully. You may also eliminate activities that aren't making a big impact.

To utilize the action priority matrix, you must first rank your actions based on their effect, followed by the effort required to accomplish them.

Quick Successes

Quick Wins are actions that have a big effect while requiring little effort. They are your most appealing hobbies because they provide a high return for little effort. You should devote as much time as possible to these types of activities.

Taking out the garbage is an example of a fast victory. It is important since it contributes to the cleanliness of your surroundings. It also deters bugs. It simply takes a few minutes to complete, which makes it a speedy victory. You won't grow bored of picking up a bag of garbage and carrying it outside, but it will undoubtedly make your house or workplace a lot cleaner.

Another example is eating a nutritious breakfast. Your health is vital, as is your energy use. In only a few minutes, you can make a nutritious breakfast. It is a critical chore that you can quickly do and will provide you with significant rewards.

Projects of Importance

Major activities are those with a high effect and effort score.

Projects. They provide excellent profits. Regrettably, they are also time-consuming and need a significant amount of work. As a result, a single large endeavor might drown out several little victories. That is something you should bear in mind while making a timetable.

Exam preparation is essential because education is essential.

College students often strive for excellent marks, which may be attained via study. It may, however, require a significant amount of time and work.

Major initiatives at work involve meeting with prospective customers to give a sales presentation. You must put forth a lot of effort to create a favorable impression.

Stand-ins

Fill-Ins are activities that have low effect and effort ratings.

You should not be concerned about these actions. You may do them whenever you have spare time. When a more appealing project comes up, you may either abandon it or outsource it to others.

Doing the laundry and watching TV are two examples of fill-in activities. Doing the laundry is crucial, and it borders on a fast victory, but you don't have to do it yourself. You may take your garments to the dry cleaners if you are short on time. If you still have enough clothing, you might even postpone this chore until the next day.

Fill-in jobs in the office include organizing interviews and responding to meaningless communications.

Unappreciated Tasks

Thankless Tasks are actions that have a minimal effect yet a high effort level. You should avoid engaging in these types of activities as much as possible. They provide little return, but they consume a lot of your time and energy that might have been spent on fast victories.

Thankless jobs include watching television and monitoring social media updates if your work does not include social media.

What can you do if vital duties continue to be pushed aside by more urgent and important activities? You must consider if it is really necessary. Do you truly have to do it, or do you just believe you have to? If it is critical, you should consider outsourcing it to other skilled individuals.

Chapter 10
Clearing your thoughts

A crowded mind is one of the most powerful adversaries of willpower.

When your mind is congested with a variety of things, it is difficult to maintain attention and concentration on the things that need to be focused on.

As a result, cleansing your thoughts becomes a crucial element of your life's maintenance routine. Indeed, cleansing your mind is comparable to detoxifying your body, only that this detox is for your mind rather than your body.

When you clean your mind, you force undesired ideas and thoughts to go. These unwanted visitors take up home in your head.

They poison your self-discipline as they put themselves at ease. These beliefs make it almost hard for you to get control of your emotions, ideas, and general motivation.

You can cleanse your thoughts using two techniques: awareness and meditation.

Both of these strategies are often misunderstood. Most people think that mindfulness and meditation are the same things since they both entail relaxation and breathing techniques.

The truth is that they are comparable because they both promote mental clarity. However, the methods they use to do this are very different.

Let's see how mindfulness works.

Mindfulness celebrates the "here" and the "now." This implies you must learn to live in the current moment. It sounds a lot simpler than it is. In truth, we are unduly preoccupied with the past and the future. But, when you think about it, the past and future don't exist in the slightest.

Sure, memories make up the past. Some are excellent, while others are not. Holding on to memories, on the other hand, is one of the most draining activities you can engage in. They sap your vitality and fill your head with things you can't control. After all, do you know anybody who could alter the past?

The same is true for the future. The future does not exist since it has not yet occurred. That is, we cannot worry about something that may or may not occur. In this instance, you must anticipate and prepare for what may occur. But, beyond that, you can't think about the future.

When you put too much emphasis on the future, you lose out on what is occurring right now. Needless to say, this will cause you to miss out on some of life's most incredible moments.

In terms of meditation, your capacity to imagine yourself attaining your goals is a terrific technique to calm your mind. You may play out situations in your head and see how they play out. You may see yourself as prosperous, traveling, or gaining goods.

You are meditating when you picture yourself doing anything.

In what way?

You are removing unpleasant ideas and replacing them with ones that you want. What this does is allow you to genuinely comprehend what you want to gain out of life.

As a result, if you can imagine yourself attaining your goals, you will get the most out of your meditation.

So, shut your eyes and relax in a comfy chair. Take a deep breath and allow yourself to disengage from your surroundings. Put away your phone and social media. They'll be there, ready to greet you. Make the most of your "here" and "now" moment.

Chapter 11
Making Things More Pleasurable and Fun!

One of the interesting facts that may continue to drive you to become more disciplined is that individuals who master these talents tend to be happy in general! Self-discipline isn't only about avoiding things that make you feel momentary better; it's also about being able to resist things that make you feel worse in the long run. Disciplined individuals can look farther ahead and recognize that acting on a whim generates a chain reaction of undesirable results, each

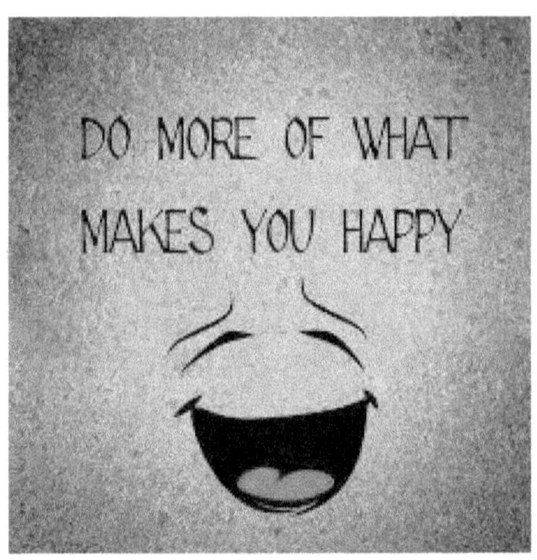

of which has a feeling of loss of control and reduced satisfaction.

Disciplined individuals may distinguish between two opposing desires: the urge to accomplish a difficult activity and the impulse to stop and do pleasurable activities.

According to research, there is a substantial association between people who accomplish projects and can remain focused on those duties and those who are more satisfied in life. This seems to be self-evident since such individuals also tend to achieve things that better their lives. According to research, the capacity to stick to activities involves being less influenced by negative emotions and spending more time feeling good or tranquil.

These folks were not better at resisting impulses or temptations, but rather at building a life that did not present as many of those temptations in the first place. They were better at designing a life that didn't involve such desires, diversions, or destructive behaviors. Instead of merely "being tougher" than others, folks who are disciplined simply avoid circumstances that clash with their stated aims.

But what if you thrive on having fun? Let's include it in your objectives as well! Nobody said that discipline had to include pain and sacrifice with no gain. We merely need to eliminate incentives that become diversions for ourselves.

Begin by compiling a list of the types of incentives you appreciate. After you've listed the things that make you happy, ask yourself:

• Do they ever distract you from your objectives, like a piece of sweets while you're trying to lose weight?

• Do I find it difficult to regulate this if I participate in it?

If you respond yes to any of those two questions, you will get short-term benefits that will develop into long-term diversions. If they don't distract, go ahead and utilize them! One example is the Pomodoro method, which we discussed before. If you aren't prone to overeating, you may enjoy a reward after each designated period. If you still desire the prize, divide out a certain amount and store the remainder far away from where you are working. If social media is your reward, create a new timer for your reward period and commit to stopping when the timer expires. If you test a reward and you can't stop or remain distracted, it's time to make it your FINAL ending prize after the assignment is completed. In this manner, your labor is already done, and since it is a one-time incentive rather than something you do frequently until the assignment is completed, it may be simpler to regulate.

You may also discover that the precise things that inspire you are also enjoyable!

Motivation is often a good sensation accompanied by a rush of enthusiasm. Is it necessary for you to view inspiring videos every day?

Who do you follow on social media who inspires you? Listen to tunes that make you feel inspired to work or finish an exercise as you work? The good thing about encouraging oneself is that it does not exhaust your energy! The exact things that drive you may serve as a springboard for you to finish your responsibilities daily!

Never forget that the result of your labor will be rewarded, but this may also be true daily. When you can go out and have fun after doing activities that make you feel successful, it is even more of a reward! If you see devotion and discipline as inspiring and energizing rather than draining and painful, you will find it considerably more enjoyable and simpler to accomplish! It all comes down to the positive internal perspective that you like your job and can accomplish difficult tasks.

Chapter 12
How Does the Human Mind Work?

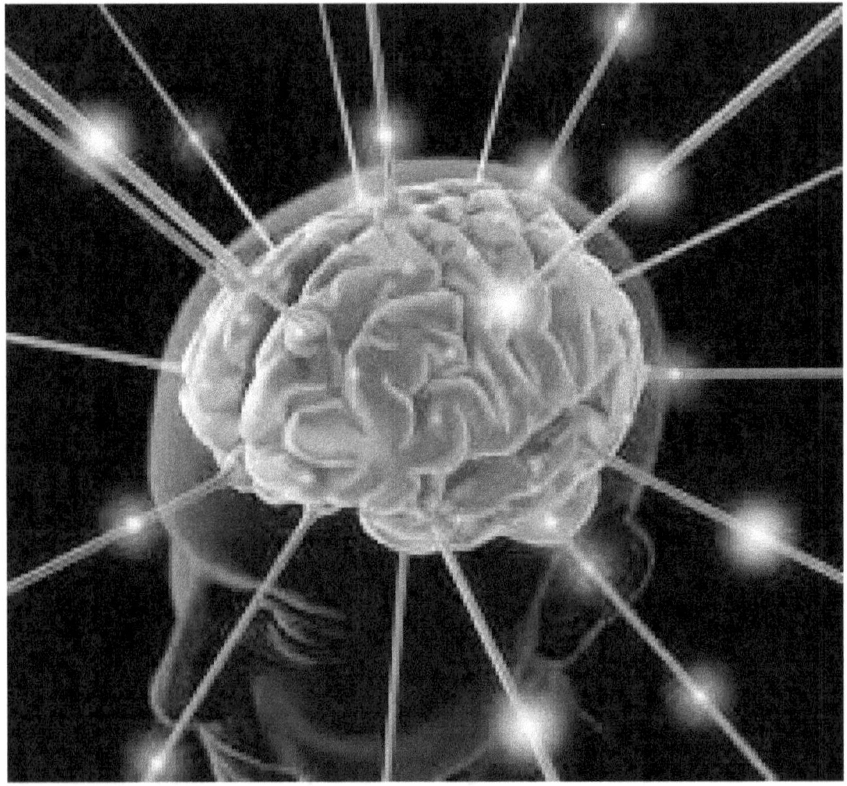

Both our conscious and unconscious minds are involved.

Friends and relatives would utilize your awake and aware thinking to determine who you are. This is the outcome of how you live your daily life and your responses to various events. This does not, however, imply that this is the region that controls your mind and all of your body's functions.

Your consciously aware mind is also a tiny piece of the brain's operations, similar to a ship captain perched on the bow spewing instructions. It is the captain's principal obligation to ensure that the crew carries out the commands given to them. This is what the unconscious accomplishes for the body and mind, and the subconscious is in charge of relaying instructions. The captain is the principal person in charge of guiding the crew aboard the ship and is the one who issues all commands for the crew to obey. However, the crew is largely responsible for carrying out the ship's commands and responsibilities. This is an excellent illustration of how the subconscious and conscious minds collaborate to manage the body.

The consciously aware mind may transmit your personality and needs to surface, which communicates the inner voice, as well as physical acts, drawings, and writing talents. Your mind is the control mechanism for memory recall as well as interface with the ongoing unconscious resources. The mind will utilize your unconscious as a station to store all memories from previous events. This process may be slowed down by traumatic events, as well as by blocking you from remembering things that are unpleasant to you. These memories are still available, but they have been unconsciously suppressed so that they do not affect you. Because of these experiences and memories, you might create habits, beliefs, and behaviors that will serve as the basis for the rest of your life.

While the conscious mind is digesting and sustaining the person's activities, the unconscious mind will communicate constantly. This connects you to your intentions for every contact you have in the world. This will enable the development of a filtered habit and belief system that transmits the proper emotions, dreams, feelings, sensations, and fantasies.

The Mind Is Always Activated

You will be able to facilitate how the three different portions of your mind function in sync to build the person that you are and how your actions work using this example.

Consider how your mind is analogous to a laptop. The ideal image to conceive for your consciously aware mind would be the keyboard and monitor. Knowledge is entered information that is typed into the keyboard, processed, and shown on the monitor screen. This is how the mind interacts with the conscious and unconscious processes — information is received from both external and internal sources of stimulus. This may include your actual surroundings as well as the

behaviors going on around you. This is subsequently processed by the brain's neurons and delivered to the conscious mind, where actions are carried out.

Your subconscious functions in the same manner that RAM does in your computer. RAM is the exact spot inside a laptop that contains the applications and information for those who are unfamiliar with computer components. Its purpose is to keep the computer running. It is much faster than other types of memory, such as disc or read-only storage.

Although your subconscious is a separate part of your mind, it functions in a very similar manner. Any present reminiscences will be placed in a hold position, allowing them to be remembered at a quicker rate since the mind is already holding them for swift recall. This is shown by your ability to remember your sign and name quickly and readily when requested. It preserves the everyday functions that you need, including behaviors, sensations, routines, mental patterns, and even the required facts for daily tasks.

Your unconscious functions similarly to the disc drive in your laptop. This serves as a repository for future recollections. It also contains the programming that occurs from birth through death.

Your mind will then use all of the programs to develop your belief system and assist you in digesting the knowledge you acquired for safety and survival from events. The two brains will then use reasoning to collaborate to assist you to survive the events and circumstances that will occur throughout your lifetime. It offers suggestions for dealing with problems and then delivers unpleasant, erroneous, and useless outcomes that may be used in various situations.

The Mind's Conscience

If you ask the general people to define what the consciously aware mind is, you will get a wide range of responses. Some argue that the capacity to be aware in your mind is what divides the subconscious from the unconscious. However, the assumption that the subconscious has no consciousness is not correct. There is a lot of evidence that the subconscious is influenced by its environment, and that consciousness may be discovered inside the subconscious as well. This is shown by a person's memories when under anesthesia.

Similar to what would happen if you drove to a distant location only to arrive with no remembrance of the journey or even how you got there. In instances like these, your subconscious will be fully attentive and will execute the activities required to keep you alive and securely deliver you to your objective.

Another prominent argument, presented by various people, is how the mind is consciously aware of what you are doing. It can instantaneously link with all of your logical ideas and reasoning. However, this does not completely separate the unconscious from your subconscious. The capacity of your mind to remain unconscious while storing memories of the past, emotions, feelings, and habits, and then connecting them with logic and reasoning for instant recall, is evidence in and of itself that the conscious and subconscious are constantly vigilant.

Consider the times when you were a child. Your mind's consciously aware components would not be completely matured yet, and they would need to be conditioned to store information about the world, people, and life. Thus, at this point in life, the subconscious mind is operating in the background while your subconscious and unconscious regions of your mind are processing information and determining the distinctions between a bottle and a toy. This line of thought distinguishes that the bottle might be a source of nourishment, that crying can get you some attention, and that a hug from mum or dad equals safety. During the early stages of life, the two brains collaborate to develop the reasoning patterns linked with the ideas, emotions, and behaviors that relate to survival and safety.

This is the simplest reasoning discovered among the two brains. It is the most powerful function, and it develops your consciously aware mind to manage the following functions:

1. The mind's capacity to concentrate on a single task.
2. The mind's capacity to link the implausible with the imaginable.
These are the two most important skills that will change your life.

Purposefully Focusing Your Direction

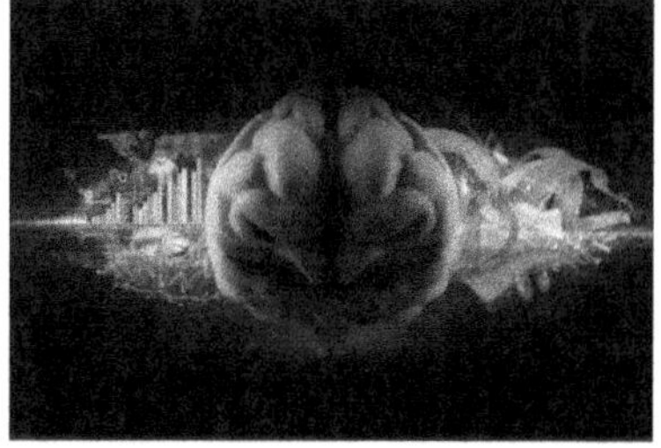

Your thoughts will be engulfed by the senses, providing a more acute awareness of the environment in which you live.

This raises consciousness of the conscious surroundings. Many people think that here is where the "sixth sense" lives and that it may be activated. This may be useful when you are both asleep and aware. It will just change the instructions that come from the mind's consciously aware part. If you deliberately direct your mind, consciously, toward negative ideas, your subconscious will send forth thoughts, perspectives, sentiments, and emotions that are of the same mood. The law of attraction operates in this manner. Whatever you concentrate your attention on is what you will always see in your reality. This produces sentiments that evolve into dread, negativity, worry, and a variety of other mental health-related emotions that complicate living.

Consider this: if you go to bed late at night and it is dark, you may hear sounds that would otherwise be inaudible.

Pay attention to anything that goes "bump" in the middle of the night. Though you allow these noises to elicit imagined terrors inside your house, you are enabling bad ideas to easily pass through your mind, even if you know there is nothing in your home.

This is caused by your subconscious, which is sending your worries and concerns into your imagination to produce unpleasant emotions. It is your mind's method of enabling your subconscious to protect you when you are in a circumstance that triggers the fight or flight response. The positive side of logical cognition is on the other end of the spectrum. This is where your conscious mind focuses your attention so that you may have a more calm and sensible reaction to events in your life, including those bumps in the night.

Often, people will discover a very easy and natural approach to focusing their positive ideas to build a more optimistic way of thinking about life. This changes their perspective on their life events and enhances their relationships with others. It is very dependent on how you sort through your prior programming, which is deeply embedded in your subconscious as well as an unconscious area of the mind. This might influence a person's thinking to be more gloomy or hopeful. You might experience pleasure as well as rage when you have negative or good mental processes. The individual may be fully in the center and have no feelings at times. Working on recognizing the method that you lean toward might help you take the first step toward changing your thought processes.

This skill allows you to command the consciously aware regions of your mind for concentration and attention. You may use your awareness to change your lifestyle and the connections you maintain by using your awareness. It enables you to keep the way you handle these ideas, as well as those relating to individuals in your life and the experiences you've had.

But how is this accomplished? The capacity to divert your attention is simple. Determining what you will do during the day, the thoughts you will have, and the acts you will allow from your subconscious can assist you in creating your destiny. This may have an impact on your good or negative thinking patterns when employing these ideas for constructive acts, as well as detrimental ones that can stifle your development and mentality inside the subconscious.

Our ideas determine how we live our lives and the obligations we accept in our surroundings. A person may be physically free of restraints, but they may be psychologically imprisoned, and the health circumstances under which they live may be detrimental to their future advancement. This will assess your determination and perseverance. We alone tend to choose the attitudes with which we live; we may modify our lives and choose our pathways. It is the path we choose that will define our outcome.

Make use of the creativity that has been bestowed on you.

Another essential skill for your consciously aware mind is the explicit capacity to employ imagination, which is useful in healing and changing your thinking. Through the power of suggestion, your mind may conceive something that is not happening and try to bring it into your reality. Your subconscious, on the other hand, is capable of providing an independent interpretation of the memories that have prevented you from letting go of previous events that have caused pain and injury to you.

But the most interesting trick that comes to mind is the subconscious mind's capacity to distinguish between genuine and fictional pictures inside the mind's imagery. This permits consciousness to be separated into two parts: imagination and actuality. These ideas may then be combined to produce emotions and sentiments that are directly tied to the visuals that are exhibited in your mind.

An example of this would be your preoccupation with being with a certain special person in your life, the excitement you feel when you think of them, and the joy of seeing their face. Then you may observe the responses you have when you think about that other person and spend time with them. These images are formed in your mind's eye as a result of these ideas. Even if you are not physically there with this person, you will feel the emotions, sentiments, and relationships as if they are. Because your subconscious thoughts have been reporting that you are experiencing these scenarios, your mind is transmitting signals of emotions and sentiments that are directly related to the specific situation. It certainly is a magnificently beautiful present that offers us unending delight!

Visualization allows us to achieve fantastic things in our lives. In one scientific research, three teams were put through a test to see whether they could improve their free throw basketball shooting accuracy by a certain amount of time. Each subject was tested both when the experiment began and when it concluded. One of the groups was taught how to physically apply the practice of free throws for a total of twenty days in a row. The secondary set of pupils was not permitted to be instructed in any way on how to practice free throws. The third group of students continued to spend twenty minutes per day in a state of calm while using visualization methods to visualize themselves and improve their free-throwing technique. They also got instruction from the teacher, who advised them to envision the free throws connecting perfectly to the hoop and then seeing themselves winning the point. They received no more instruction.

At the end of the research, the instructors tallied the findings and discovered that those who physically exercised had improved their free throws. Those who employed visualization improved significantly, while those who did nothing to enhance their score had little improvement. Individually, the increase for those who anticipated winning was a staggering 23 percent, which is equal to the aggregate sum of the first group's improvement. This implies that the mind's potential to alter your life via simple imagery is underappreciated.

The subconscious mind may help you make positive changes in your life.

As previously said, your subconscious thinking can impact the changes that occur in your personal life as well as your physical appearance. Many individuals have practiced and studied visualization methods to bring about genuine improvements in their lives. The alterations that may be made range from dramatic to insignificant. This might range from eating healthier to creating a whole new self.

The subconscious mind's involvement in your life will be spectacular.
Your subconscious will operate in tandem with the functioning of your regular activities outside of your short-term memory region. This implies it is critical to your capacity to live an active life. It laboriously works with particular components of your mind to speed up remembering and make access to your ideas simpler to handle.

Things that are comparable to the list below –

- Memories — for example, earlier experiences, such as driving your automobile. Because you have already learned these things, you can do this intentionally without having trust in your talents. This might also involve the look you want to attain from your home's surroundings.

- Current activities that you engage in daily, as well as the behaviors you display and your mood or routines.

- Filters related to beliefs and value systems- These are used to analyze data that is evaluated for validity as they occur. This maintains the balance between perception and reality. Similar to the senses you've cultivated through time: sight, touch, smell, and hearing. This allows you to discern between the true sensations and filter out the ones that have been offered to you.

If you have difficulty filtering these sensations, you may employ a frame of reference to store the data in your subconscious. This is what RAM does for the computer system. It enables you to utilize the unconscious to access the programs associated with these senses, allowing the incoming signals to be processed by previously acquired information.

The subconscious is also always at work, paying attention to many more things going on in your environment than the normal sight would detect. In reality, when we comprehend the natural language communication paradigm for processing, we tend to calculate maltreatment every moment of the day. If your mind is aware of how to deal with issues that have arisen, you will be able to deal with them effectively without finding yourself in an unpleasant scenario. Instead, by filtering things using your subconscious, you will be able to sift out the extraneous information so that it only sends what is required for that period. This implies you can only carry 7 bits of information at a time. In a background setting, your mind is capable of doing all of these things. This gives a technique to execute jobs that are not hampered by the work that is done regularly. Based on previously programmed knowledge that has access to the unconscious, the mind may process these activities rationally and methodically.

The connections that exist inside the subconscious

When it comes to the subconscious, we can rely on it to follow our commands. People mistakenly believe that the subconscious controls the mind; however, this is not correct. The precise opposite is a more accurate response. You influence your subconscious and how it guides your life. You will be the one who decides what to do and how to accomplish it. That is why many individuals are taking charge of their own lives and achieving significant success. Your awareness gives you the guidance you need to achieve your dreams, and then you digest the progress stages. When you employ the subconscious correctly, you may supply feelings and emotions via an infinitely productive belief system.

Now, I am by no means an expert in language and attitude, but it is as easy as altering your ideas and the words you use to shift your whole life path. In most circumstances, your default applications have an overwhelming amount of energy attached to them, allowing them to change in a flash. Although it may not be a fairly abrupt alteration in your life, it will reappear inside the programming if a big life-altering event has occurred or if enough pain is associated with the prior behavior.

The capacity of your brain to operate

Your brain, like the mind, attempts to cope with a remembrance of a prior event. There is, however, differentiation between each segment. You can imagine the human mind if you contemplate the picture of a constellation. By seeing the human mind as a constellation, you may also envisage a layer deeper, which is the unconscious mind. The subconscious mind is one layer deeper. This is similar to observing the constellations inside the solar system before moving on to the galaxy. Although these systems of conscious thinking are causally connected, they vary in numerous ways. They also have an impact on different but related thoughts in your mind. This indicates that the brain is the basement, and the subterranean library is the desires and reminiscences of a bygone era. This also applies to the habits that are developed, as well as the behaviors that accompany those habits. The mind is the storehouse for all of the emotions that are deeply ingrained inside you as a result of your birth programming. If you need to make changes to your core level, here is the place to do so. Although it might cause very unpleasant and rapid outcomes.

The function of your subconscious mind in your life

In many ways, using the unconscious mentality will deal directly with ongoing activities relating to subconscious memories, sentiments, habits, emotions, and behaviors. The unique link will bring the two brains together; however, the subconscious is the mentality area that gives the programs that are in use.

It is also the only spot that will function with memories and events that have occurred since your birth. This is where ideas, behaviors, habits, fashion, and strengths will be remembered throughout time.

How to Make Positive Lifestyle Changes

If you want to make fundamental changes to your lifestyle, you should force yourself to apply these exact measures to the present programming. This programming is intended to regulate your activities and lifestyle. Other measurements may be changed for more specific modifications. These will assist you in recreating incidents that occurred over your lifetime. This will help you to adjust your perspective of the events and see them in a new light, allowing you to change your lifestyle. This occurs in both the subconscious and conscious consciousness.

By feeling guilty about the bad ideas you allow to govern your lifestyle and mistreating the visions in your mind, you are preventing yourself from living a fulfilling, happy, and positive existence. These programs are constantly in control of how you conduct your life. By using these mindset reframing tactics, you will begin to see a shift in the concepts that your unconscious is cognitively carrying about as useful material and belief systems.

And as soon as this occurs, you will have a deeper degree of knowledge modification! It is a popular strategy. These behaviors, habits, and beliefs, on the other hand, have been methodically cultivated inside this area of your mind from birth. This allows you to modify them, but it may take some effort and determination to see genuine changes. However, bear in mind that the travel should be enjoyable for you!

What are paradigms and how do they impact brain results?

Humans have around 7% of all-time low neuron relationships compared to any other animal. As a result, astrocytes have one of the highest ratios at 76 percent. Einstein, a well-known scientist, was recognized during his lifetime for having the all-time lowest ratio for neurons inside the brain, which meant he also had the greatest ratio for astrocytes of all persons examined. If you can read and then form assumptions about the content, your brain is working at a far greater neuron rate than Einstein's.

Repetition is used to program your subconscious.

So, focusing on happy ideas rather than negative ones may be a difficult trip. However, repetition allows you to train your brain.

It is a question of what ideas you let flow through your mind. This unlimited intellect has given you the power to govern your thoughts properly. The irony is that the majority of individuals do not readily utilize such judgment.

It is a simple formula, but not the simplest. As a consequence, applying all of these ideas requires on-the-fly implementation. Many of you may be ready to completely rewire your mind based on the weight you assign to your positive beliefs. I know that if you just think good things for many weeks, your capacity for development and transformation will increase enormously.

If you believe you will fail, your thinking will ensure that you do. This is the outcome of your subconscious satisfying the expectations you place on it. You may begin to influence your outcomes by adopting a more optimistic frame of mind. You will begin to create changes that will affect your whole life and future by employing positive reinforcement and thinking.

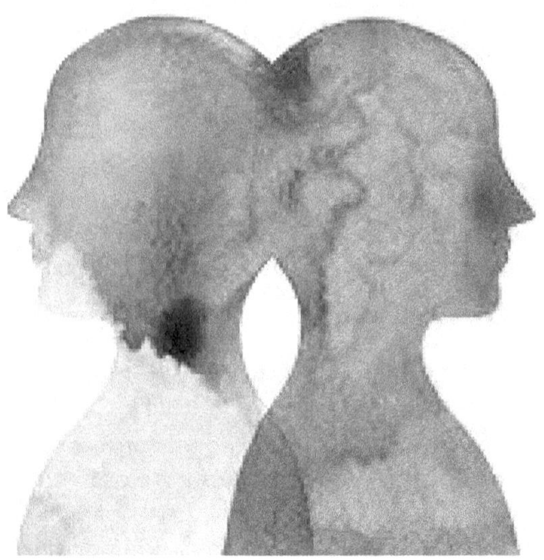

Chapter 13
Uncertain Beginnings and Complicated Plans

Have you ever been asked to perform something and, just as you were about to begin, discovered that the directions were unclear, leaving you confused about how to proceed?

Worse, have you attempted figuring it out on your own? You felt awkward going back to the person who requested you to do that thing because you didn't want to seem stupid or incompetent? How much productive time did you lose as a consequence, if you did? I'm sure that was a lot.

Being unsure of how to begin and proceed with your chores or assignments can push you to delay. Why? Because you'll need time to figure out how to begin doing the things you need to do and how to continue to finish them, especially if you're the type who is hesitant to ask for more detailed instructions on how to complete your assigned tasks and responsibilities for fear of being judged negatively. If the instructions and anticipated outcomes are unclear, the temptation to postpone to discreetly find out how to do your given chores becomes quite great.

It's similar to action movies when the heroes take their time before flying a chopper they discovered to safely escape from their foes. Often, the heroes don't know how to fly a helicopter or a spacecraft - depending on your preference - and must figure it out on the fly. It takes a long time for them to do so, which raises their chances of being captured or killed. But, since it's the movies, the heroes usually figure it out just in time and fly the chopper or spacecraft to safety.

But you don't live in a movie, and your odds of figuring things out in the nick of time are often minimal, so it's preferable to ask for clearer instructions and expectations directly from the individuals who assigned the responsibilities to you. By directly asking them, you avoid the need for trial and error and the wasting of valuable time in clarifying instructions and expectations. You get started right away and prevent procrastination in the process.

More than mere procrastination, confusing starts may significantly raise your odds of doing things incorrectly, which may need significant repairs or changes to your final work, extending the time of that and future activities and projects. What a two-for-one! That's why it's critical to clear things right away so you don't have to postpone and can get started on your jobs and projects right away. And how can you guarantee that all of your starts are distinct?

Pose inquiries. It's as easy as that.

Complicated plans

Another factor for procrastination is complicated plans of action for accomplishing jobs and projects. They might make it difficult for you to begin working on activities and projects right away since you may not understand how to put such ideas into action to achieve your goals.

Consider investing in Bitcoins to double your money in the next one to two years. Investing in Bitcoins or other cryptocurrencies is not as easy as it seems. Unlike conventional financial assets such as equities, bonds, or government securities, investing in Bitcoins or other cryptocurrencies is not as straightforward as it appears. For starters, cryptocurrencies are much more complex than typical financial instruments like the ones I described. Cryptocurrency investment is more sophisticated than investing in stocks and bonds due to their highly unique properties, the method in which you may invest in them, earn money from them, and their degree of financial risk. And, due to the intricacy of cryptocurrencies and the plans of action required to effectively invest in them, it's quite likely that you'll put it off and, as a result, lose out on possibilities to make significant returns on your investments.

Weight reduction is another example of how intricate plans of action may lead to procrastination. Many individuals desire to reduce as many pounds as possible in as little time as feasible. As a result, they opt for very restricted and difficult diets such as Paleo, vegan, and ketogenic diets. If you don't think they're complicated, why not look into how they work? They will have to put in a lot of effort to keep within a pretty small range of meal options, which may be complicated to adhere to if they already have a lot on their - excuse the pun - plate. And I've seen many folks put off starting weight reduction programs because the intricacy of the plans they picked overwhelmed them.

Chapter 14
Breaking Bad Habits

As we all know, laziness is a trait that almost everyone has. It is the state of not wanting to perform any labor or spend energy, more akin to laziness. Some people misinterpret it as a refusal to complete a tough or painful duty, yet laziness is independent of the severity of the activity at hand. If you are lazy, you will not bother to complete any work, no matter how simple or difficult.

Laziness is a characteristic shared by all people. Everyone feels sluggish at different periods of the day. Some people believe that laziness is a personality condition, although this is not the case. Laziness, like many other habits and behaviors, is something you've become used to. It is not a sin to feel lethargic, but it is not appropriate to spend the whole day being lazy. So, how can you break this bad habit of yours? So, first and foremost, what are the reasons for laziness?

- Lack of drive
- Lack of self-confidence
- Procrastination
- Distractions
- Exhaustion
- Poor nutrition
- Irresponsibility

Lack of motivation is the major cause of laziness. Many of us feel unmotivated to complete our jobs. Motivation is essential in everyone's life. You can't go ahead if you don't have even a smidgeon of motivation. Laziness may also be caused by a lack of self-confidence or a lack of enthusiasm for the task at hand.

Lack of self-confidence or self-worth implies a lack of belief in one's abilities. If you believe in yourself, you will be motivated and anxious to finish all of your chores as quickly as possible.

Otherwise, you will quickly get fatigued and sluggish. Procrastination may also lead to laziness. As you are all aware, procrastinating is the act of postponing or delaying a job that must be completed. The only reason you put off work is that you are lazy. Laziness increases the amount of labor that must be done, and you may end up not avoiding the job. So, constantly remember not to put off work out of laziness. Distraction is also a major source of laziness.

You might be sidetracked in a variety of ways. Electronic gadgets, social media, chatty individuals around you, and thinking about exciting/upcoming events are the most prevalent sources of distraction.

Another reason for laziness is exhaustion or fatigue. Being engrossed in too much work and arriving home late, fatigued and drained, may cause you to be sluggish for the remainder of the day.

Laziness may also be caused by a lack of nourishment. If you do not eat a well-balanced diet, your body will not have the energy to execute all necessary duties. A well-balanced diet does not contain carbonated beverages, fried chips, or junk food. A well-balanced diet includes more fresh vegetables, fruits, and other high-nutritional-value foods. Not eating the correct foods for your body causes weariness, which leads to laziness and other serious problems. Being reckless is also a contributing factor to laziness.

The majority of the time, irresponsible individuals are lazy. If you are irresponsible, you will not bother with work and will instead sit idle.

Too much labor may sometimes be a source of lethargy. When you have too much work, you tend to slow down over time, leaving you drowsy and unable to continue. Because you are overburdened with work, your brain becomes exhausted and confused. You may now have a better understanding of the reasons for the sluggish behavior you've developed.

How can you tell whether you're feeling sluggish or if laziness has become a habit in your daily life? So, consider the following questions.

1. Do you sleep for a longer period than usual?
2. Do you feel exhausted even after a full night's sleep?
3. Are you dissatisfied?
4. Are you concerned about anything?

5. Do you have an excessive amount of tasks to do?
6. Do you find it difficult to inspire yourself to complete your work?

If you answered yes to these questions, laziness has become a habit in your life. If you are not joyful, anxious, or fearful about anything, you may as well be sad, and this is what is causing you to be sluggish. This is a significant problem that must be resolved as quickly as feasible. Laziness is often a behavior that we have developed for ourselves. As a result, we won't have too much trouble getting rid of it. However, if the sluggish behavior is caused by depression, it may be more difficult to break. As a result, you should seek the advice of a qualified physician. However, if your depression is caused by personal difficulties or terrible friends, you might attempt talking to them to remedy the situation or avoid them if necessary. If it doesn't work, seeing a doctor is the best and safest option.

Being a little lackadaisical for a day is not a sin and will not cause a major problem.

However, if it is something you do regularly, it might complicate your day. This may lead to major problems, worry, and anxiety.

Worse, it may become a habit, which is undesirable. You will be able to break the habit of being lazy if you understand why you feel that way. It all depends on why you're feeling sluggish.

Here are some strategies for dealing with laziness.
• Determine the root cause of your lethargy;
• Plan your daily routine;
• Reward yourself regularly;
• Believe in yourself; and
• Organize yourself and your surroundings.
• Have someone keep an eye on you.
• Seek counsel from successful individuals.

First and first, determine the actual source of your laziness: is it a lack of drive, a lack of self-confidence, distractions, bad nutrition, a heavy task, or something else? If you can figure out why you're doing it, you'll find it much easier to break the habit. It would be difficult to eliminate this behavior if you do not understand why you have it. There is a cause for your sluggishness. So, figure it out and figure out how to get rid of it. Making a plan for your day might also help you overcome your lethargy. This strategy may be useful for folks who are feeling lethargic as a result of procrastination or having too much work to complete. Make a schedule for your day, including times of day and lunch breaks. You will be able to do your task more effectively and without stress or strain this way. You will become more organized and responsible as you grow used to such a routine.

Your worry and dread will diminish as well.

Rewarding oneself is another interesting technique to combat lethargy.

Because no one is going to thank you regularly, why not do it yourself? Plan a particular amount of work to be completed within a given time frame, and if you finish it on time, reward yourself with one of your favorite beverages or a few minutes of amusement. In this manner, you'll be motivated to complete your assignment as quickly as feasible. Believing in oneself can also greatly assist you in overcoming lethargy. Have faith in your ability to do the assigned work within the time frame, and keep encouraging yourself. Make a vow to yourself before beginning your assignment that you will not be distracted by anything and that you will finish your work within the time frame.

This way, you won't want to violate your commitment and will work hard to accomplish your assignment without distractions or laziness.

You will undoubtedly succeed if you believe in yourself and your abilities. Another strategy to combat laziness is to arrange yourself and your environment. You may feel sluggish if your surroundings are disorganized. Maintain a clean, tidy, and well-organized environment in your house and surroundings. This will motivate you to stay occupied and not simply sit around. A tidy and well-organized environment can help to keep your mind calm and free of unwelcome thoughts and lethargy. Furthermore, not only must your surroundings be clean and nice, but so must you. An uncomfortable and filthy environment will only muddle your thinking, leaving you confused and worried, causing you to feel lazy and not bother with any of your pending jobs.

Having someone keep an eye on you is another good strategy to stay on track. You might choose a few friends or family members who are willing to leave you a message or phone to see whether you are performing your job. Make sure the few individuals you pick can inspire and encourage you to achieve your assignment in any way.

The last option is to seek guidance or learn from successful individuals. This kind of person will be able to inspire and push you to focus on your job entertainingly and break negative habits, laziness, and procrastination. Aside from the long-term efforts indicated above, you may attempt a few basic steps to keep yourself on track. Follow these easy steps to feel more energized and think more optimistically.

- Do not do your work indefinitely. Take frequent pauses and keep moving forward.
- Set aside time for meals. You don't want to miss meals since it will lead to health concerns.
- Make a plan or schedule for the day. Even if you are unable to do everything as specified, strive to adhere to the plan as much as possible.
- Participate in certain physical activities, such as sports or workouts. Your mind will be calm as a result, and you will be able to focus on your task much better.
- Try doing something you like during your breaks or free time. You may have interests such as reading, gardening, watching television, and so on. So, why don't you spend your free time doing one of these?
- Remind yourself of the advantages of finishing all of your tasks on time. You will undoubtedly face problems and hardships in your job, but remind yourself of the rewards and advantages of finishing your assignment, and this will keep you focused on your work in any case.
- Get adequate rest. A few hours of sleep is insufficient and will leave you exhausted and drained throughout the day. Our bodies need at least 6 hours of sleep to remain healthy and steady during the day. It is usually difficult to work till late at night. If this is the case, you might sleep early and set an alarm to get up early in the morning to complete your task.
- Remind yourself of the ramifications. You will almost certainly run into problems if you do not accomplish your assignment appropriately and within the time frame specified. So constantly remind yourself of the repercussions, and you'll be motivated to do your assignment as quickly as possible.
- Never miss breakfast. Make an effort to have breakfast on time. Breakfast is the fuel that keeps you going throughout the day.
  You will be unable to focus on your task if you do not have breakfast, and you will get fatigued and drained soon.
- Concentrate on one task at a time. If you have a lot of work to accomplish, do it one at a time. Do not attempt to do it all at once, since this will jumble things and leave you puzzled. It is preferable to accomplish each duty one at a time. Order the tasks and do them one at a time.
- Stay away from procrastination. One of the primary reasons you are finding it difficult to accomplish your assignment is procrastination. Do not get used to this habit, which will cause you to be sluggish regularly. Never put off doing your task; instead, do it as quickly as possible and

then relax. It is always best to enjoy yourself once you have finished your job since you will not be able to enjoy yourself as much if you have a lot on your mind.

- Try to avoid using electronic gadgets for a short period before going to bed. If you go to bed immediately after using your phone or laptop, your mind will not be calm and will be filled with those ideas. Allow yourself and your thoughts to unwind.

Getting rid of laziness is a difficult endeavor. But if you give yourself a push, there is nothing that you cannot do!

Chapter 15
How to Avoid Procrastination

Avoiding procrastination looks to be extremely tough while you're in the throes of procrastination; in any case, it's not difficult to avoid procrastination if you begin your tasks with the right mindset. Anyway, how would you go about doing this? How would you avoid procrastinating in the first place? Continue reading to find out!

In this approach, being compulsively determined to achieve your objective is the major strategy for avoiding procrastination (s). When you're pushed to do something, it's difficult to put it off since it's at the forefront of your mind and you can't stop thinking about it. When do you have time in your schedule to procrastinate?

Unfortunately, not everyone can be compulsively motivated to do the duties that must be completed. Furthermore, if you are not encouraged to that degree, it is usually easy to delay for several reasons.

Procrastination concerning sluggishness occurs only sometimes. For example, I often suppose I'm too lazy to even consider going to the shop; in any event, if you dig a little further, you'll discover there are many causes why you put things off. My area isn't ideal for this issue, and when I go to the shop, I often have to avoid off-break sellers and too persistent homeless individuals in transit in and out, even though it's not precisely a square from my house...

Overall, while you're delaying, ask yourself, "for what purpose am I procrastinating?" Consider the "additional benefits"; after all, how can you avoid procrastinating? For example, what benefit does it provide you if you delay your task till the last minute?

For some people, a dreadful deadline is beneficial to their work process since the pressure and anguish of failure compel them to work. This occurs because individuals are strongly convinced by the prospect of avoiding discomfort. It's not difficult to put off writing the paper until a couple of hours before it's due since writing may be a painful process; in any event, it's less unpleasant than failing a class or being fired from a job.

In any event, even in this model, you can see that procrastination is often based on more than one problem region. For example, you may look into why you don't like the work of writing. Or, on the other side, why isn't the satisfaction of completing chores greater for you? Is procrastination motivated by a desire to split hairs? (It's simple to set yourself up this way: venture has a deadline, yet if I begin today, I'll need to do it flawlessly and won't have enough energy to truly finish... however, if I put it off, I'll simply need to do what's available.)

On the other side, you may apply a method that I used to overcome this problem myself: I set short, strict deadlines for myself, so I normally need to finish things in all respects quickly and with an abnormal level of accuracy. This allows you to use the tool that causes you to postpone achieving your goals.

Procrastination: Why and How to Overcome It

Everyone has procrastinated at some point in their lives.

Procrastination is especially appealing when faced with a challenging assignment. However, putting off jobs or endeavors is unreliable and works against a person's ability to be profitable and fulfill his or her greatest potential.

Figuring out how to win Procrastination is the only way to get enough time on the board.

Why Should You Overcome Procrastination?

Procrastination suffocates productivity. Everybody has to do a few things every day, and procrastinators often postpone tough activities (which are frequently the most important ones) until the last possible moment. This may have an impact on the quality of the job produced.

Inconvenience is caused by procrastination. Procrastination prolongs one's sorrow. It takes away precious time that a person would have spent undertaking haphazard workouts.

Procrastination erodes your self-esteem. Most procrastinators put off starting work because they don't believe they can complete it.

Procrastination foreshadows personal growth. Procrastinators spend the bulk of their time working without really accomplishing anything. If a person had the choice of finishing his or her task on time, the person in question would have done many things to help better themselves.

Overcoming Procrastination: Step-by-Step Instructions

Familiarize yourself with the art of order. When people are distracted from what they should be doing, the great majority inadvertently loiter. Learning self-control will allow a person to resist distractions and focus on the work at hand.

Consider motivation when you begin working on your assignment. Taking up a full-time job is a good way to start beating Procrastination. Many individuals only become aware of their depression after they have taken the first steps.

Create your certainty. Dithering to undertake tough work is sometimes caused by a lack of self-assurance. Some individuals second-guess their ability to perform a job and postpone it until the last feasible moment. Having faith in oneself is a fantastic first step in defeating Procrastination.

Follow the plan for the day. Plans are developed to ensure that a person completes the duties for the afternoon. If anything unexpected occurs, keep an eye on it while remaining on course.

Remember to appreciate a respite. When planning, short breaks should be supplemented regularly. People need pauses from time to time to inhale and re-energize their thoughts and bodies to do another work. A large reward at the end of the day also discourages procrastination since it encourages the individual to finish his or her task on time.

Procrastination, in general, is only a state of mind that everyone can overcome. If you want to start hesitant, consider a suitable motivation. Working power will help you finish a job in the long term. You may also take a break to clear your head, then return and try again. Furthermore, you might think of something to look forward to towards the end of the day to help you focus on your assignment and complete it on time.

Putting an End to Procrastination

Why does procrastination put you under pressure?

Another common but inescapable source of anxiety in today's culture is procrastination, or constantly putting off the completion of duties.

Procrastination is seen as a stressor since it commonly leads to postponements and forces individuals to pack at the last minute. Procrastination in this manner results in a slew of increasingly unpleasant outcomes.

Procrastination can take several forms:

People lament 99 percent of the time after they procrastinate because they have less time to finish what they should have started earlier.

While delaying, a person may feel content and joyful; nevertheless, it's a different story when due dates begin to loom, and the slacker realizes that he has officially spent a big chunk of his available time.

What causes individuals to procrastinate?

To overcome procrastination, we must first understand why people do it in the first place:

Performing easier tasks before tackling the more difficult ones.
Choosing enjoyable workouts over more important exercises.
Playing out a series of less important exercises so you don't have to start from scratch.

1. **Discomfort -** It is a well-known truth that every major endeavor or activity involves some level of discomfort. It is necessary to devote effort and spend energy on something to achieve significant outcomes.

When a person has a low tolerance for mental, emotional, or bodily pain, he may delay avoiding experiencing discomfort.

The most frequently accepted reason for postponing certain workouts is a low threshold. People are often unaware of their discomfort thresholds; hence, the choice to postpone is motivated by an innate desire to avoid pain.

2. Fear of Failing - Some adults are so afraid of failing that they put off getting things done for as long as they can.

When a person anticipates disappointment, they envision all of the mental and emotional discomforts that they would experience if they do not succeed in completing a work nicely. People who believe in compulsiveness are prone to procrastination due to a general fear of disappointment.

3. Fear of Rejection - There are a few instances where a physically fit adult is reluctant to do something because he believes that someone (almost like a professional figure) will object to their activities.

This dread is founded on the notion that other people's appraisals are far more important than your own.

For example, a person who has required to learn how to paint may postpone indefinitely because they fear that others would judge their works of art as average or bad.

4. Refusal to Do Something - When a person believes that it is inappropriate for them to complete a task, they will generally refrain from completing the task for as long as possible.

As the deadline for the assignment approaches, a person may get more perplexed and enraged. When they have to work twice or three times as hard to complete the task, the individual may become increasingly concerned about the situation.

1. **Don't Overthink** - Overthinking anything is never a good idea since it is debilitating to cycle identical thoughts in a single's mind more than once while never relying on activities.

Rather than thinking about doing something over and over again, do what has to be done. Remember Nike's slogan, "Get it done?" It's the ideal trademark for avoiding procrastination!

2. **Modify Your Mindset -** Many people procrastinate to postpone discomfort or strain.

Rather than thinking that you are freeing yourself from any discomfort, consider procrastination to be a source of trouble because you will end up remembering all of the things you need to do, even if you aren't doing them right now.

3. **Plan Ahead -** If you are concerned about the outcome of something you need to do, you can reduce your anxiety or questions by making a plan ahead of time. Make a note of the specifics of what you need to do as well as the overall scope of your project.

Normally, we view things differently when they're written down. Items that seem to be horrible or too difficult to handle and supervise appear to be less difficult to control and oversee when you record the specific details if this works for you then repeat this approach whenever you feel like postponing.

If at least one of the reasons stated above bothers you, remember that they are mostly mental states that you may intentionally override for progressively pleasant and lucrative behavior.

Chapter 16
10 Time-Saving Hacks

Procrastinators who seek perfection are another sort of procrastinator. They put off starting the job until the last minute.

Even when they are just getting started on the project, they whine about not having enough time to finish it. When they postpone a task, these procrastinators usually come up with fantastic excuses.

That is one of the characteristics of procrastination that we have previously addressed.

You may be busy and have a lot to accomplish, but overworking is not the way to become a productive person or prevent procrastination. When individuals fail to meet deadlines, they attempt to blame the deadline, yet it is evident that the deadline has nothing to do with their failure. It is all their fault since they procrastinated. However, most individuals seldom accept it.

You will not be able to work with a comfortable mentality if you wait until the deadline. You will not be able to perform at your best if you are not in a calm state of mind. Focus on your objectives if you don't want procrastination to come your way. Make sure to separate your objectives in a manner that allows you to attain them. Also, keep in mind that if you do not comprehend the importance of your objective, you will not hesitate to postpone it.

If you want to attain your objectives, you must first recognize their worth. People may delay because they lack self-confidence and believe they will be unable to complete the allotted activity. However, just thinking about it causes them to postpone their job and adds to the strain. Then they begin to question if they will be able to accomplish the assignment on time.

I am not suggesting that you become a productive person immediately after reading this book since that is not feasible. However, you must make one adjustment at a time. Procrastination may be overcome by being proactive.

Accept the truth that you dislike working under duress.
Some individuals, such as attorneys, emergency room doctors, and politicians, genuinely prefer working under duress (no pun intended). That's fantastic if you can accomplish any of these things! You're misguided if you believe you're exceptional at working under pressure. The underlying cause of your overwork is that you have postponed the work, and you must task hard if you want to finish the project. Furthermore, you do not want to underperform, which is why you believe that you work better under pressure. The only choice you have is to not put off doing an assignment until the final minute.

Don't be afraid to use the Pomodoro Technique.
This strategy has previously been addressed. You may manage your job by using this time management strategy. You will work for 25 minutes and then rest for 5 minutes.

You may use this strategy anytime you have a job that has been postponed or when you are allocated a large assignment. Instead of thinking, "I'd have to spend my whole life to complete this assignment," you might say, "I'll use the Pomodoro Technique." It will help you keep concentrated if you know you just have to focus on a segment for 25 minutes and then you may take a five-minute break. This is one of the most effective strategies for getting things done.

Do your best.
For example, you may be required to create an eBook. The book must then be divided into chapters. You will feel more in control if you have split the chapters. Furthermore, there may be some chapters that are simple and others that are tougher. However, due to the degree of complexity, not

everyone can work. As a result, if you feel like doing the first, just write. Don't assume you have to accomplish the difficult ones first and then the easier ones. It doesn't work like that. You must do all in your power!

Make a choice.

You must designate someone to follow up with you if you fail to fulfill the deadlines. It might be your parents or friends, but you must answer them. You might ask them why you haven't fulfilled a certain goal you set for yourself. However, that person must be firm and consistent with you!

You should not multitask.

You may have been misled into believing that multitasking is advantageous. But believe me, it is not! When you multitask, you tend to lose focus on all of your duties. Of sure, some individuals can multitask, but if you are not one of them, you should avoid doing so. You will jeopardize the quality of all your work by multitasking, which will lead to more problems. Furthermore, it may cause you to delay your task. Instead of multitasking, you may focus on one job at a time and perform your best for that activity.

Exercise

If you believe that exercising when you have work to complete is a kind of procrastination, you are mistaken! When you don't have enough drive to achieve anything, it's simple to get sidetracked. It's simple to avoid doing it. As a result, if you are not in the mood to work, you will postpone.

Instead of delaying, consider concentrating on some exercise.

The activity will increase your endorphin levels and make you happy. You may discover numerous workouts online, so look for several and save them. Exercise might help you feel better when you're feeling down or unproductive!

When you postpone, you are guilty.

Even though we all delay, when we confront the repercussions, we tend to feel bad about it. There may have been moments when you lost out on a lot of fantastic perks just because of your procrastinating tendency. And there will be days when you have to work all night to fulfill a deadline. There may be occasions when you must abandon friends to complete the assignment before the customer becomes enraged.

Consider all of these scenarios and embrace the truth that you are a procrastinator. Once you accept this, you will be able to gradually conquer the problem. Acceptance is also the most effective method to get things done.

Consider the outcome.

What will happen if you put this work off? What may be the worst outcome of postponing this project? Procrastination, as I have said, is related to fear. You may utilize this fear to your advantage when it comes to procrastinating. How? It is rather straightforward. You just need to consider the consequences of postponing a project. Consider your boss's furious expression or a colleague's disappointed expression. Consider the repercussions of postponing the project. And when you do, you will naturally be afraid of the mess you will make. As a result, you will attempt not to postpone the task. The concept of using fear to your advantage will assist you in avoiding procrastination.

Give yourself a great treat.

Small incentives may not always fulfill your need for recognition. Also, if you are better than previously at avoiding procrastination, you should lavishly reward yourself. After you finish the job, you must determine what you want to do. And the burning desire to have fun will improve your job and make you more productive.

Simply do it.

"JUST DO IT," as the popular phrase goes, because you have to do it! It's your project and your duty. You have accepted responsibility for doing it, therefore you cannot evade or find excuses not to do it! One of the most typical reasons for procrastination is a lack of motivation to accomplish the activity. Why don't you want to finish the task? The answer is irrelevant since if you have accepted the work, you are accountable for doing it, so just do it! You must comprehend the reality that you have accepted labor. As a result, you must do it. Allow it to sink in.

If it does, you may find yourself not waiting until the last possible moment to accomplish a job.

That being said, getting things done is entirely dependent on how you think! Your thinking is the driving force behind getting things done. Think. Perform. And triumph!

Chapter 17
Your 7-Day Plan to Quit Smoking

Today's Procrastination

Now that we've spent some time discussing procrastination and how it may harm your life, it's time to devise a strategy to halt procrastination in its tracks. This strategy will assist people who have realized that procrastination has progressed from something they do on occasion to something they do daily. It will provide you with some basic measures you may follow over the next week to reduce your procrastination so you can finally get things done.

You should focus on each of the following elements for this strategy. Consider incorporating them into your daily routine if feasible. Most of them will not take long, and if you can execute them regularly, you will see the greatest effects. If you want to divide things up even further (another idea), work on each portion one day a week. The overarching idea is to incorporate all of them into your everyday routine so that you may eliminate procrastination and achieve results.

The 5-Minute Rule

The five-minute rule is one of the things you should follow this week. It
will completely change
the way you do things
daily and ensure that you
can win the battle against
procrastination. The five-
minute rule requires you
to ask yourself what
action you can do right

now or later today that will take five minutes or less and will propel you ahead
in life. It makes no difference how far ahead it carries you; all that matters is
that it advances you at all.

When you've identified this kind of task, get a timer and set it for the five
minutes you'd want to work. Then get to work for the duration of that period.
Anyone can sit down and work for five minutes, so toss away all of your
excuses. The great thing is that studies have shown that once you start
anything, you are more likely to complete it. As a result, although you may
start with five minutes on that enormous report at work, once you get started,
you are more likely to stay with it and complete more, if not all, of the job.

The Zeigarnik effect is what makes this work. Unfinished chores,
according to this impact, are more likely to get ingrained in your memory.
Your mind is probably locked in a loop over all of the tasks you haven't been
able to finish. Even if you are busy and just have a few minutes to work on
that assignment, it will now be ingrained in your mind, and you are more
likely to complete it. Even the smallest action will catapult you ahead. If you
have the time, you could do the assignment in five minutes. If you're too
busy, at least you've begun it and it's in your memory to work on later.

Make time for a Power Hour.

This might be a terrific approach
for you to focus only on your job and
begin something you've been putting
off till now. It just takes an hour of
your time, so it's simple to fit into your
schedule, but you'll be surprised at
how much you can get done in this
time, as well as the amount of
inspiration you'll discover if you stay

with it. Set aside an hour for each day of this seven-day strategy and name it your power hour to get the task done.

So, what should you do during this power hour? During this time, you will begin by removing any distractions and then work for focused periods. As a novice, it is advisable to work for around twenty minutes at a time so that you may complete three sessions in an hour. You will take a brief pause between each of these sessions to give your brain a breather from what you are doing.

This may seem to be paradoxical. You may believe that taking breaks will slow you down and make it difficult to get anything done, but alternating bursts of concentrated work with short breaks, even if they are only five minutes away from the computer screens and the work you are doing, can help you get the most performance out of your brain. You'll get a lot of work done, and you could even consider incorporating this kind of power hour into other sections of your day so you can catch up quickly.

Allow Others to Set Your Deadlines

When you have to set deadlines on your own, it might be difficult to remain impartial. You may believe that you have more time to work on something or that it will not take you long to complete a task, but you may be mistaken. Sometimes you need extra time to complete a task, and other times you may be much too kind to yourself. This is why having someone else set the deadlines for you might be beneficial, at least in the beginning while you are learning the ropes and getting rid of your procrastination.

Find someone you can trust and ask them if they can check at some of your projects and recommend timeframes that you should fulfill. Put those deadlines on your calendar and stick to them no matter what. This will assist you in completing the assignment on time and maybe a fantastic approach to keep yourself responsible.

Determine which tasks should be completed first.

Prioritizing the work that needs to be done will make a significant impact on how much you get done throughout the day. You may feel like you're getting a lot of work done throughout the day if you're fooling about with some of the minor tasks during the day, but you're still not getting to some of the major projects that need to be done.

To begin with this one, you must first create a list of all the tasks that must be completed. This covers everything, whether you have to do them now, later this week, or in a month. Make a list of everything, no matter how essential it is, so you don't forget anything.

Once you've compiled this list, it's crucial to prioritize which ones need to be addressed immediately away. Choose a highlighter color and use it to make a list of everything you need to do that day. These include tasks that are due in the next few days, items that will take you a little longer but that you want to get started on, and so forth. This section of the list will most likely just have a few items highlighted, but these are the ones you need to do as quickly as possible.

Now, choose another highlighter color and highlight all of the tasks that must be completed soon but have less time and are not as critical as the other items on the list. Items such as those due towards the end of the week, rather than those due tomorrow, might fall under this category.

Finally, you may choose a third color to indicate all of the remaining chores that you can do later. When it's time to get to work, you may proceed down this list, completing everything in the order of the colors you choose until they're finished.

You will need to revise this list every day, adjusting which things are most essential depending on where you are in the week and adding additional items as you need to work on them. As you move through the list, strive to get as much done as possible each day, but concentrate your concentration on the tasks deemed the most critical.

Choose the Best Time of Day to Work

Everyone has a particular time of day when they get the most work done. For most individuals, starting their job first thing in the morning, before they are fatigued and worn out, is one of the finest choices they can make. Many individuals, though, function best in the late afternoon or evening. Whatever time works best for you, try to plan your day so that you can concentrate your attention on getting things done during that time.

When you attempt to work outside of your peak hours, you will waste a lot of time. Nobody can get a lot of work done when they are not at their top, and this may derail your drive.

On the other side, if you discover what your peak period is and concentrate the majority of your work time during that time, you will be able to breeze through the job without feeling like you are working as hard.

Even if you have never considered it, you most likely already know when your peak time is. Consider the periods when you can get the most work done when it does not seem like you have to put in as much effort. This is the moment when you should be at your best. If you don't know what your peak time is, it's time to do some experimenting. Experiment at a few different times of the day to discover when it appears to work best for you to get a lot of work done.

Once you've determined when you need to complete your job, make sure that you plan your day around that peak time each day when you get into the office so that you can get a lot done. It makes no difference whether your peak period is in the morning, around noon, or later in the day. Make a timetable for everything else so that you may work on it during this period.

Reduce Your To-Do List

You should also think about condensing your list. Hopefully, you've discovered that making a list of everything that has to be done throughout the day will help you never forget anything again. However, as you look at this list and watch it grow over the week, you may notice that it is becoming somewhat lengthy. Long to-do lists are uninspiring to everyone. Sure, it feels good to cross items off the list as they are completed, but looking forward and seeing a lot of work that has to be done is not encouraging.

After you've completed your list, the first thing you should do is figure out what you can eliminate. There are always items on every list that you can eliminate. Is there an activity planned for the kids throughout the week that you may skip if things become too hectic? Are there any personal projects that you'd want to do but don't believe will fit in now that you've seen what else has to be done? Are there any responsibilities at work that you can delegate or at least ask someone else to assist you with?

If you can reduce this list even somewhat, it will make a significant impact on how motivated you are to do the assignment. The job will seem more doable, and you may even be eager to get started. But first, you must choose the best strategy to reduce the size of that list.

Once you've whittled down your list, work hard to maintain it that way. It's not going to help you much if you cross off a handful of items from your list and then add ten more from work or other sources. This will be difficult for some people who dislike telling others no, but it is necessary for beating your procrastination. Only choose to take on jobs that you are capable of doing, and the rest will fall into place.

Learn about your distractions and how to avoid them.

Several distractions might hinder you from completing your assignment.

Whether you are constantly checking your phone, reading emails that pop up when a new notification arrives, or constantly on your social network account, certain distractions are there and keep you from performing your job. You may even believe that you are putting in a lot of effort on a project when, in fact, you are primarily wasting your time with little diversions.

If you want to get some work done, you must eliminate any distractions. Turn off the phone and put it in the desk drawer or on the other side of the room. Instead of checking email or social media accounts first thing in the morning, go to work on your tasks. Keep the door locked so that none of your employees may walk in and interrupt you unless they have a specific need. The key here is to identify your distractions and then avoid them as much as possible.

It is difficult to break the habit of being distracted once it has been ingrained in your everyday life. You've become so accustomed to it that when someone brings you a new assignment, your first reaction is to put it off until later; however, if you include some of these basic tips into your everyday life, you'll discover that you're well on your way to combating procrastination and reclaiming your life.

Conclusion

The process of transitioning from impulsive procrastinator to goal achiever entails an internal transformation that involves learning and development. This contributes to the transformation of who we are, how we see ourselves, others, our situations, and how we interact with the world around us.

If you're still unsure where to begin, try these tiny suggestions to get you started:

Choose at least 5 tasks that you can do tomorrow. You can push through practically anything if you are determined to achieve change and showing to yourself that you are competent. Begin with 5 tasks, even if they have nothing to do with your ultimate aim, and do them within 24 hours.

To remain in the present moment, begin with positive thoughts and awareness. Nothing is more damaging to your ambitions than negative thinking and self-sabotage. You can never go wrong by learning how to control your thoughts. Even if you don't start living a disciplined life right once, you may change your emotions and thoughts right away with a new emphasis.

One of the most important things you can do to truly change your habits from laziness to discipline is to approach the change with a positive addition mindset rather than a punitive subtraction mindset. That is, instead of thinking about something you are giving up or letting go, think about something you will add to your day. People who regard their eating habits as adding more protein or providing more nutrients via leafy greens are more likely to modify their eating habits. They see an increase in control or the capacity to feel better after eating.

Approaching change from a positive, adding standpoint causes you to feel as though you are getting rather than losing.

Those who approach change by focusing on what they must give up, such as time or "favorite foods," feel starved.